Cookbook for
COLLEGE K

Graduation Guara

A revised classic for the novice cook

*Cooking
is like love,
IT should be
entered into
with abandon
or
not at all!*

By
Sheila McDougall, B.H.Sc.

Front cover — skillet chicken niçoise, page 78

Cookbook for College Kids
by:
Sheila McDougall, B.H.Sc.

Fourteenth Printing – June 2001

Copyright © 1978 by
Sheila McDougall, B.H.Sc.
2207 Sirocco Drive S.W.
Calgary, Alberta, Canada   T3H 2T9

Canadian Cataloguing in Publication Data

McDougall, Sheila, 1931-
   Cookbook for college kids

   Rev. ed. of: Something special cookbook for college kids.   1981.
   Includes index.
   ISBN 0-919845-56-8

1. Cookery.   I. Title.   II. Title: Something
special cookbook for college kids.

TX715.M33 1988   641.512   C88-098018-4

Editorial work: Pam McDougall
Cover design: Rhae Ann Bromley
Illustrations: Wayne McDougall
Photography by:
Ross C. (Hutch) Hutchinson
Hutchinson & Company Commercial Photography Ltd.
Calgary, Alberta

Dishes and Accessories Compliments of:
Benkris & Co., Calgary
Fabulous Things Giftware Ltd., Calgary
The Happy Cooker Emporium, Calgary
Marcel De Paris, Calgary
Market Kitchen, Vancouver
Pot Pourri Kitchen Shoppe, Calgary

Designed, Printed and Produced in Canada by:
Centax Books, a Division of PrintWest Communications Ltd.
Publishing Director, Photo Designer & Food Stylist: Margo Embury
1150 Eighth Avenue, Regina, Saskatchewan, Canada S4R 1C9
(306) 525-2304   FAX (306) 757-2439

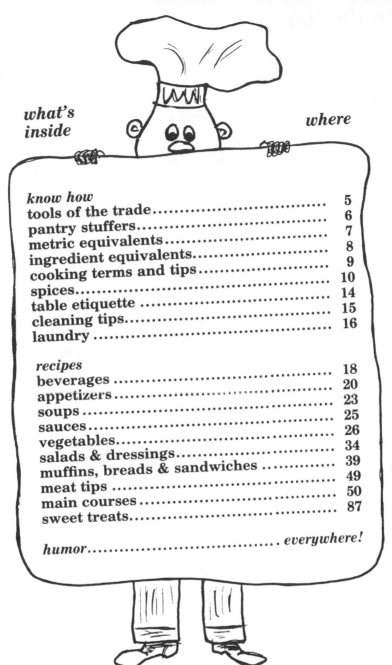

what's inside   where

Recipes marked with Ø are easily halved - pan sizes and cooking times should be adjusted accordingly and writing in new measurements for all ingredients is advised.

The recipes in this cookbook have all been tested in the standard measurements only. The metric equivalents are given for those cooks who are more comfortable with metric.

introduction

Welcome to the revised "Metric" edition of "Cookbook for College Kids".

This collection of recipes and cooking hints has been put together to assist students (and others who are just setting up housekeeping) to perform culinary tasks with some degree of confidence. No prerequisites are necessary to master these recipes - just a little time, common sense, spirit of adventure and sense of humor. My better judgement told me to leave the "honeydew soup" recipe for the experts and I refuse to share my recipes for burnt chicken giblets, burnt hard-cooked eggs and flaming turkeys!

From one busy person to another - here is the "know how" to help you over the hurdle of putting a delicious meal on the table in a minimum amount of time and with maximum ease and efficiency.

Your cooking career is about to begin! No longer will you fall in the door after school, work, fitness class or whatever - feeling starved and frustrated about what you are going to cook for dinner.

Now that you have the desire and determination to cook easy, appetizing and nutritious meals in spite of your busy lifestyle (and your addiction to eating out) - I sincerely hope that your cooking will be fun with "Cookbook for College Kids".

I am most grateful:
- to friends and relatives who shared their favorite recipes.
- to the retailers and distributors for their support and friendship.
- to Rhae Ann Bromley for our exciting new cover design.
- to Margo Embury (of Centax) for her patience, sense of humor and expertise. It was a great pleasure and learning experience to work with you.

A very special thank you "WITH LOVE" to my husband for the delightful "chef" designs and cartoons and to my entire family - for your encouragement when I needed it most - your honest opinions, advice and constant enthusiasm. This book would never have been completed without you.

4

tools of the trade

essential:

bread board
bread knife
paring knife
chopping knife
carving knife
spatula
can opener
bottle opener
wooden spoon
measuring cups
measuring spoons
mixing bowls
egg beater
grater
wire strainer

desirable:

scissors
vegetable peeler
grapefruit knife
tongs
vegetable brush
rolling pin
pastry blender
electric mixer

top of stove cookery

2 or 3 saucepans (with lids)
kettle
frying pan
coffee pot

double boiler
teapot
splattershield for
frying pan

oven cookery

muffin tin
cookie sheet
8" (20 cm) square pan
pie plate
loaf pan
roasting pan with rack
assorted casseroles
9 x 13" (23 x 33 cm) baking
pan

meat thermometer
microwave oven!!
slow cooker (electric)!

pantry stuffers

for cupboard:

all-purpose flour
baking powder
baking soda
bread
breakfast cereal
chili powder
cocoa
coffee, tea
crackers
curry powder
garlic salt or garlic powder
hot chocolate
macaroni
mustard, dry
mustard, prepared
potatoes
rice
salt and pepper
seasoning salt (Lawry's)
spaghetti
sugar, brown
sugar, white
vanilla
vegetable or salad oil

for refrigerator:

cheese
eggs
fruit
honey
jam
juice
ketchup
margarine or butter
mayonnaise
meat
milk
onions
peanut butter
relish
vegetables

paper supplies

foil paper
kleenex
paper lunchbags
paper towels (expensive -
  use sparingly)

sandwich bags/plastic wrap
toilet paper
toothpicks
wax paper

scrub-a-dubbers!

soaps - laundry, hand, dish
powdered bleach
S.O.S. pads
comet

dish and pot scraper
sudsy ammonia - fantastic for
windows, walls, floors, etc.
  (NOT for rugs)

shopping hints

1. never shop when you are hungry.
2. use lists, plan ahead but be flexible.
3. buy foods in season.
4. check for specials.
5. buy in large quantity if practical.

approximate standard/metric equivalents:

volume

				rounded
			=	5 mL
1 tsp.	=	1 tbsp.	=	15 mL
3 tsp.	=	1/4 cup	=	50-60 mL
4 tbsp.	=	1/3 cup	=	75 mL
5 1/3 tbsp.	=	1/2 cup	=	125 mL
8 tbsp.	=	1 cup	=	250 mL
16 tbsp.	=	2 tbsp.	=	30 mL
1 fl. oz.	=	1/2 cup (1 gill)	=	125 mL
4 fl. oz.	=	1 cup	=	250 mL
8 fl. oz.	=	2 cups (1 pint)	=	500 mL
16 fl. oz.	=	4 cups (1 quart)	=	1000 mL (1 L)
32 fl. oz.				

weight

	=		=	30 g
1 oz.	=	1/4 lb.	=	125 g
4 oz.	=	1/2 lb.	=	250 g
8 oz.	=	1 lb.	=	500 g
16 oz.	=	2 lbs.	=	1000 g (1 kg)
32 oz.				

oven temperatures:
250°F = 120°C
300°F = 150°C
350°F = 180°C
400°F = 200°C
450°F = 230°C

baking dishes:

standard	metric	standard	metric
11 x 7 x 1 1/2"	28 x 18 x 4 cm	8-cup	2 L
13 x 9 x 2"	33 x 23 x 5 cm	14-cup	3.5 L
8 x 8 x 2"	20 x 20 x 5 cm	8-cup	2 L
9 x 9 x 1 3/4"	23 x 23 x 4.5 cm	10-cup	2.5 L

jelly roll:			
15 1/2 x 10 1/2 x 3/4"	39 x 27 x 2 cm	8-cup	2 L

pie plates:			
9 x 1 1/2"	23 x 4 cm	4-cup	1 L
10 x 1 3/4"	25 x 4.5 cm	6-cup	1.5 L

simple but true: — when you want to know the volume of a casserole, simply use cups or litres and fill with water!

ingredient equivalents:

1 lb. (500 g) butter	= 2 cups (500 mL)
1 stick butter	= ½ cup (125 mL)
1 lb. (500 g) shortening or lard	= 2⅓ cups (575 mL)
8-10 double graham wafers	= 1 cup (250 mL) crumbs
1 cup (250 mL) raw macaroni	= 2 cups (500 mL) cooked
7 oz. (225 g) raw spaghetti	= 4 cups (1 L) cooked
1 cup (250 mL) raw noodles	= 1¼ cups (300 mL) cooked
1 lb. (500 g) cheese	= 4 cups (1 L) shredded
1 cup (250 mL) raw rice	= 3 cups (750 mL) cooked
1 cup (250 mL) quick cooking rice	= 2 cups (500 mL) cooked
1 cup (250 mL) whipping cream	= 2 cups (500 mL) whipped
1 cup (250 mL) mini. marshmallows	= 10 large marshmallows
juice of 1 lemon	= 2-3 tbsp. (30-45 mL)
1 cup (250 mL) fresh egg whites	= 8-10 whites approx.
1 cup (250 mL) fresh egg yolks	= 14-16 yolks approx.
1 lb. (500 g) dates	= 2½ cups (625 mL) pitted & chopped
6 oz. (170 g) chipits	= 1 cup (500 mL)

substitutions:

1 cup (250 mL) cake flour	= 1 cup (250 mL) all-purpose flour less 2 tbsp. (30 mL)
1 cup (250 mL) self-raising flour	= ¾ tsp. (3 mL) baking powder plus 1 cup (250 mL) all-purpose flour
1 tbsp. (15 mL) cornstarch (for thickening)	= 2 tbsp. (30 mL) flour
1 tsp. (5 mL) baking powder	= ¼ tsp. (1 mL) baking soda plus ½ tsp. (2 mL) cream of tartar
1 oz. (30 g) sq. unsweetened chocolate	= 3 tbsp. (45 mL) cocoa plus 1½ tsp. (7 mL) butter
1 oz. (30 g) sq. semisweet chocolate	= 2 rounded tbsp. (30 mL) chipits
1 cup (250 mL) sour milk or buttermilk	= 1 cup (250 mL) milk plus 1 tbsp. (15 mL) lemon juice or vinegar
1 cup (250 mL) butter	= 7/8 cup (200 mL) lard or shortening
1 tsp. (5 mL) dry mustard	= 1 tbsp. (15 mL) prepared mustard

for the adventurous chef:

Sweet Sherry	for	Marsala wine
White Rum	for	Kirsch
Dubonnet	for	Madeira

8

cooking "savoire faire":

— when cooking with meats, vegetables or cookie dough, here are some terms you might like to know.

á la king — food served in rich cream sauce
au gratin — with a crust, sometimes with cheese
baste — to moisten by spooning liquid over foods
blend — to mix 2 or more ingredients until well combined
breaded — to dip in egg wash (1 beaten egg plus 1 tbsp. [15 mL] water or milk) and then in seasoned bread crumbs
brioche — slightly sweetened rich bread
en brochette — cooked on a skewer
chutney — a spicy relish made from fruits and vegetables
compôte — a mixture served in a stemmed dish
cream — to stir and beat until soft and smooth
cut — to cut fat into a dry mixture with knives or pastry blender
dredge — to coat with thin coating of flour or sugar
dust — to sprinkle lightly with flour or sugar
fold — to blend 2 mixtures by cutting down through mixture with spatula, turning over and under until all is blended
glaze — to cover with glossy covering
julienne — food cut in narrow lengthwise strips
knead — fold dough firmly towards you with palms of hands, press down, turn dough and repeat
lyonnaise — seasoned with onions and parsley
macedoine — a mixture of fruits or vegetables, cut or sliced into various shapes
marinate — to tenderize or season by covering with highly seasoned sauces, wine, etc.
parboil — to precook slightly in liquid
poach — to cook in liquid just under the boiling point
ragoût — highly seasoned thick stew
reduce — to lessen amount of liquid by boiling it away
roux — melted fat and flour mix
sauté — to cook in small amount of very hot fat
scald — to heat liquid to just below boiling point
score — to make shallow cuts in a surface
sear — to cook quickly at high temperature
simmer — to cook in liquid kept just below boiling point
tortilla — a thin, round Mexican bread
truffle — a creamy chocolate candy or specialty mushroom

*Which Spice
Where
How Much*

— *dried herbs and spices are more concentrated than fresh*
— *suggested formula for substitutions try:*
  ½ tsp. (2 mL) dried = 1 tbsp. (15 mL) fresh, then add more if desired
— *spices are used to enhance the natural flavor of foods. Use sparingly when experimenting with new ones, especially hot ones such as cayenne, curry, chili powder.*

bouquet garni — *basically refers to a combination of bay leaf, parsley and thyme tied in a cheese cloth - used in soups and stews.*

suggested seasonings to try:

allspice — *stewing chicken, soups, cakes, cookies*
basil — *(crushed leaves) tomato, fish, eggs, mushrooms, new potatoes, salads*
bay leaves — *soups, fish, pot roasts, corned beef*
celery seed — *dips, salad dressings, meat marinades, fish sauces, poultry stuffing*
cloves — *an onion studded with whole cloves is great in a soup pot*
curry — *use with discretion, can be hot - sauces, poultry dressing, lamb, chicken, eggs*
dill weed — *salads, vegetables, fish, cheese spreads, sauces, dips*
marjoram — *sauces, soups, fish, stuffings, eggs, vegetables, pot roasts*
mint — *(crushed leaves) peas, potatoes, fruit salads, punches, sauces for lamb*
parsley — *sauces, soups, stews, salads*
pepper (cayenne) — *use carefully and sparingly - it's hot! - appetizers, eggs, tomato dishes, fish*
rosemary — *soups, stuffings, vegetables, lamb, veal*
sage — *poultry, pork, fish, meat loaf*
savory — *fish, salads, stuffings, poultry, meat loaf*
smoked salt — *use sparingly - hamburgers, fish, appetizers, barbecue sauces*
thyme — *tomato, soups, fish, poultry dressings, Bouquet Garni*
turmeric — *may be used instead of saffron for yellow coloring*

note — *dried spices do deteriorate over the years - take a sniff and if you don't get a distinct aroma you should treat yourself to new ones - expensive but worth it!*

best brain food
— *your daily eating pattern should include the following:*

a. **milk & milk products**
   — 2 servings per day
   — e.g. milk,
   milk puddings,
   yogurt,
   cheese,
   ice cream

b. **bread & cereals**
   — 3-5 servings per day
   — e.g. whole wheat OR
   enriched bread,
   rice, noodles,
   macaroni,
   cooked or ready-to-eat
   cereals, crackers

c. **fruits & vegetables**
   — 4-5 servings per day
   — include at least
   2 vegetables per day
   - raw ones are best!

WE'RE DIFFERENT

d. **meat & alternates**
   — 2 servings per day
   — e.g. beef, pork, chicken, fish,
   dried beans, peas, lentils,
   eggs, peanut butter

— *each food group has it's own nutrient strengths.*
   Do not interchange groups.
   A good BALANCED diet makes a healthier,
   happier YOU!

The hardest part of dieting is watching your friends eat!

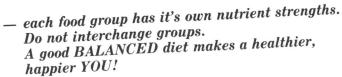

did you know:

— to measure ½ egg, you just beat the whole egg and use half of the mixture.

— egg whites beat up best if they are at room temperature. Traces of egg yolk should be removed (half an egg shell will take them out better than a spoon!).

— to soften brown sugar, add a slice of bread to your container.

— cold water is a "NO-NO" on hot pots or pans.

— to mash garlic cloves, peel them first, then mash with a fork.

— minced garlic may be purchased in jars (a time and money saver).

— cheese likes to be stored in plastic wrap (and served at room temperature!).

— when melting chocolate, grease your pan first for easier cleaning.

— to replace a cork in a bottle, cut a wedge out of the cork.

— when making sandwiches for the "brown bags", they will be better if you forget the salt (salt will make lettuce wilt).

— to freeze leftovers - line a casserole or pot with foil leaving 4-6" (10.2-15 cm) overlap. Fill with food, wrap well, label and freeze. When frozen, remove casserole (saves dishes and freezer space!).

— when recipes suggest you sauté vegetables or meat, etc. in butter or margarine, I usually use half vegetable oil - butter burns quickly!

what you can freeze (other than meat and vegetables):

— coconut, marshmallows, grated cheese, egg whites, popping corn, bread, buns, bananas (to use for baking), nuts.

what not to freeze:

— canned hams, cooked egg whites, salad dressings (unless only small amounts used in mixtures), gelatin-based dishes and cream pie fillings.

— about freezing leftovers - do so as soon as possible for best results.

words for the wise:
— Try to be a creative, imaginative cook - don't ignore a recipe if it calls for green peppers and you don't like green pepper. Leave out the mushrooms if you don't like same or sprinkle them on top where you can see them and avoid them. Learn to substitute, within reason. After all, chili needs chili powder just as bread dough needs yeast. If you don't like cream of mushroom soup, use cream of celery or chicken instead. Get the idea? You'll be amazed at the results - most of the time!!

about menu planning:
— if you are planning a personal specialty dish for a meal, select simple easy courses for the supporting roles.

— think color! Steamed fish with mashed potato and cauliflower does little to stimulate the appetite.

— consistency is another factor - scalloped potatoes enjoy crispy vegetables for company rather than creamed peas.

— consider your oven temperature. If cooking several items in the oven, the oven temperature required should be similar.

— start your preparation for a meal by preparing whatever dish will take the longest to cook.

— anyway you do it - enjoy yourself and remember - "Cooking is fun!".

time well spent:
You will do yourself a big favor if you read recipes thoroughly before starting and double check that you have included all ingredients (a cake without the baking powder would be a flop!).

table etiquette
— in case you've forgotten what your mother tried to teach you!

— *glasses are placed in the order that they will be used.*

— *flatware is also placed in the order it will be used.*

— *blades of knives face the plate.*

— *guest of honor - if a lady - sits to the right of host; - an honored gentleman - sits to the right of the hostess.*

— *all dishes are served to the left and removed from the right.*

— *beverages are served to the right.*

traditionally

— *red wines are served at room temperature.*

— *champagne, rosé and white wines are served chilled.*

— *dry wines are served before sweet.*

— *white wines are served before red.*

— *light wines are served before heavier.*

— *white wines accompany fish and white meats.*

— *red wines accompany dark meats, game and cheese.*

— *dessert wines are served at room temperature.*

Wines like to be stored in a cool dark place. Corked wines should be stored lying down so that the cork does not dry out.

*clean is
good*

*clean is
safe*

*your hands
cooking equipment
utensils
work surfaces
food*

"Learn to apply a constant dose of everyday tidiness!"

*If in doubt
THROW it out.
Moldy, slimy, smelly foods
go out! out! out!
P.S. Bacteria LOVE wooden bread boards!*

household hassles:

— don't force sticky drawers. Rub the sticking surface with a bar of soap.

— when the drip of the faucet drives you buggy, tie a string to it, long enough to reach the drain - water should run down noiselessly (or hang a dish cloth over so it drapes into drain).

— the best way to discourage a grease fire is to throw baking soda on it!

— sprinkle salt on spills in oven - it will prevent smoking and should make cleaning easier!

— to prevent sinks from talking back, remove grease from pots and pans, etc. before washing!

— put baking soda in an open dish in refrigerator to eliminate odors!

— Polident is super for cleaning narrow-necked jars, vases, etc. (just fill container with water and dissolve a tablet in it).

— for cleaning windows, mirrors, counter tops, etc. the following recipe does a great job and saves you money too!

½ cup	sudsy ammonia	125 mL
2 cups	methyl hydrate	500 mL
1 tsp.	Sunlight OR other detergent	5 mL
	water	

Mix in a gallon (4 L) jug using enough water to fill the container. Fill your empty spray bottles. CAUTION - this is poisonous - keep away from children.

laundry lingo
— empty pockets, close zippers!

— never put dark or brightly colored clothes to wash with other clothes before testing. If color runs, it's salt to the rescue. Soak in strong salt solution of 4 tbsp. (60 mL) per quart (L) of water for 24 hours. Rinse in vinegar water.

— don't use too much detergent in washing machine.

— powdered bleach is safe for all - unless bleaching is not recommended. Liquid bleach must be added to the water first and agitated before clothes are added.

— soak dirty white socks in Bio-Ad.

— corduroy garments should be washed inside out to collect least possible lint.

— hang shirts, etc. immediately when dryer goes off.

✋	Handwashing	△	Bleach
○	Drycleaning	□	Drying
⊔	Washing	🪧	Ironing

stubborn stain savvy
— act promptly.

— avoid hot water on stains you cannot identify.

— test stain removers on hidden parts of fabric.

— work in well-ventilated room when using cleaning solvents.

— to avoid the calamity of making big spots out of little ones:
  1. place a sponge or rag under bad spot (acts as a blotter and gives spot somewhere to go).
  2. attack spot with a wet rag using cold water.
  3. feather your spot. This means to gradually blend wet place into dry place and hopefully avoid the ring that is so common a fault for would-be-successful home dry cleaners!

how to cope with specific stains — for washable fabrics!

non greasy stains on light fabrics:
— *soak with powdered bleach.*

greasy stains:
— *most can be removed with detergent and hot water. Some may require a grease solvent (available at drug stores or notion counters).*

combination stains (*both greasy and non greasy*)**:**
— *e.g. coffee with cream*
— *soak for 30 minutes in cool water. Rub detergent on, rinse thoroughly, allow to dry. If stain persists, sponge with solvent.*

chewing gum:
— *rub with ice cube or put in freezer, scrape off.*

alcoholic beverages:
— *follow above steps for non greasy stains.*

blood:
— *soak in cold water, rinse thoroughly, bleach if necessary.*

chocolate:
— *wash in hot water. Bleach may be necessary.*

coffee, tea:
— *follow above steps for non greasy stains. If it contains cream, follow directions for combination stains.*

cosmetics:
— *usually detergent will suffice - if not try cleaning solvent.*

grass:
— *you can't beat Luster Sheen (in black can, found in grocery store), rub on before laundering.*

mayonnaise:
— *follow directions for combination stains.*

mud:
— *let dry, brush vigorously.*

mustard:
— *rub detergent on, rinse. If stain persists, soak in hot suds.*

mildew:
— *treat while fresh, wash thoroughly in bleach solution.*

perspiration:
— *pretreat by soaking in solution of 4 tbsp. (60 mL) salt per quart (L) of warm water. Wash with detergent. Bleach if stain persists.*

ring-around-the-collar:
— *spray with a spray laundry cleaner before washing (available in cleaning section of grocery stores).*

red wine:
— *sprinkle with salt, soak in cold water.*

beverages

fruit slush Ø

yield: 48-10 oz. (1.36 L) servings

— So refreshing on a hot afternoon.

4 cups	sugar	
8 cups	water	1 L
2	lemons, juice only*	2 L
5	oranges, juice only*	2
2	bananas, mashed	5
48 oz.	pineapple juice	2
	7-Up, as required	1.36 L

Bring sugar and water to a boil. Cool. Add remaining ingredients, except 7-Up and freeze.

To serve, put 1 scoop, ⅓ cup (75 mL), of frozen slush in a 10 oz. (300 mL) glass. Fill with 7-Up, about ½ cup (125 mL) per serving.

* You could take the easy way out and use 4-6 tbsp. (60-90 mL) bottled lemon juice and about 2 cups (500 mL) of frozen diluted orange juice.

See photograph page 96A.

hot spiced tea Ø

yield: approximately 75 servings.

— great for chilly evenings!

1½ cups	instant tea	375 mL
1½ cups	sugar	375 mL
2 x 3½ oz.	orange Tang (2 pkgs.)	2 x 92 g
1 tsp.	cinnamon	5 mL
½ tsp.	cloves	2 mL

Mix all ingredients together. Use 2-3 tsp. (10-15 mL) per mug. Add boiling water and serve pronto!

kahlúa

yield: 3½ quarts (3.5L) liqueur

4 oz.	instant freeze-dried coffee	115 g
6-8 cups	berry sugar	1.5-2 L
4 cups	boiling water	1 L
26 oz.	brandy	750 mL
26 oz.	vodka	750 mL
26 oz.	water	750 mL
1	vanilla bean OR vanilla, to taste	1

Mix coffee, sugar and boiling water and allow to cool. Add remaining ingredients.

note: ½ vanilla bean = approx. 2 tbsp. (30 mL) vanilla.

tia maria

yield: 1 quart (1 L) liqueur

2½ cups	white sugar	625 mL
1½ cups	boiling water	375 mL
2 tbsp.	instant freeze-dried coffee	30 mL
½	vanilla bean, finely chopped	½
26 oz.	vodka	750 mL

Boil sugar, water and coffee for 5 minutes. Allow to cool. Add vanilla and vodka.

Self control is the ability to carry a credit card and not use it.

appetizers

artichoke dip

yield: 2½ cups (625 mL) of dip

— *even if you have never eaten artichokes, or are convinced you wouldn't like them, do buy yourself a can and try this. It is truly a tangy collage of flavors that will tease your appetite.*

14 oz.	can artichoke hearts, drained & chopped	398 mL
½ cup	Parmesan cheese, freshly grated	
1 cup	mayonnaise	125 mL
½ tsp.	garlic salt	250 mL
dash	lemon juice	2 mL
		dash

Mix all ingredients together. Serve with taco chips, crackers, etc.

clam dip

yield: 1½ cups (375 mL) of dip

— *may be served hot or cold - hot is yummy!*

8 oz.	cream cheese	
5 oz.	can baby claims, drained, chopped	250 g
dash	salt	142 g
dash	Tabasco sauce	dash
¾ tsp.	Worcestershire sauce	dash
1 tsp.	minced green onion	7 mL
		5 mL

Whip cheese and add remaining ingredients.

variations:
You could substitute smoked oysters, crab meat, shrimp, etc. for the clams but don't forget to change the name!

barbecue sauce or dip Ø

yield: 3 cups (750 mL) of dip

— for fondue or dipping party sausages, potato skins, etc.

		250 mL
1 cup	ketchup	250 mL
1 cup	water	50 mL
¼ cup	vinegar	15 mL
1 tbsp.	Worcestershire sauce	
1	small onion, minced	1
1	garlic clove, minced	1
2 tbsp.	brown sugar	30 mL
2 tbsp.	molasses	30 mL
2 tsp.	dry mustard	10 mL
1 tsp.	chili powder	5 mL
1 tbsp.	smoke flavoring (optional)	15 mL

Combine all ingredients in saucepan. Simmer over low heat for 20 minutes.

note: — You may want to add smoke flavoring, a bit at a time, to suit your taste!
— Excess sauce may be kept in refrigerator for 1-2 weeks.

See photograph page 80A.

dip for raw vegetables Ø

yield: 3 cups (750 mL) of dip

		125 mL
½ cup	sour cream	50 mL
¼ cup	horseradish	500 mL
2 cups	mayonnaise	2 mL
½ tsp.	seasoning salt	10 mL
2 tsp.	dry mustard	2 mL
½ tsp.	salt	30 mL
2 tbsp.	lemon juice	

Mix all together. Chill until serving time.

potato skin crisps ∅

yield: 4-6 servings

4	large baking potatoes, baked (see recipe page 28)	4
	seasoning salt (optional)	
	grated Parmesan cheese (optional)	
	chopped green onions (optional)	

Just cut baked potato in half and gently scoop out most of the pulp. Cut skins into strips as wide as you wish. Place on baking sheet and brush well with melted butter. You can also add seasoning salt, Parmesan cheese, chopped green onion, etc. Bake in 450°F (230°C) oven for 8-10 minutes until crispy. Serve with your favorite dips.

helpful hint — To use up your cooked potato, you could mix it into patties with a bit of butter or bacon fat, seasoning salt and chopped onion. Heat oil in a frying pan, add patties, brown and serve!

See photograph page 80A.

cheese and chili dip ∅

yield: 2 cups (500 mL) of dip

— *for potato skins, tortilla chips, etc.*

6 slices	bacon	6 slices
2 cups	grated Cheddar cheese	500 mL
1	onion, finely chopped	1
4 oz.	can green chilies (mild), chopped	113 g

Fry bacon, drain and crumble. Mix all ingredients together and heat, over low heat until cheese is melted.

variation:

You could also sprinkle ingredients over chips, potato skins, etc. in a shallow pan and bake in 350°F (180°C) oven until cheese is melted.

This recipe may be halved (freeze remaining chilies for next time).

See photograph page 80A.

soups

french onion soup Ø

yield: 4 servings

— the easy way!

1½ oz.	pkg. onion soup mix	40 g
1	egg yolk	1
3 tbsp.	white wine	45 mL
1½ tbsp.	cornstarch	22 mL
	French bread	
	grated mozzarella OR Gruyère cheese	
	Parmesan cheese	

Prepare onion soup as directed on package. Mix egg yolk with white wine and cornstarch. Add to soup and stir until thickened. Divide into 4 oven-proof bowls. Top with a thick slice of bread, lots of cheese and broil until slightly brown. Sprinkle with Parmesan cheese for the final touch. Serve with garlic toast (below).

garlic toast

— simply butter thick slices of French bread, add minced garlic or garlic salt and broil. Watch carefully - it burns quickly!

minestrone hodgepodge

yield: 6-8 servings

— a hearty soup - just add 1½-2 cups (375-500 mL) water* to the recipe for minestrone casserole, page 64.

* or beef broth and/or canned tomatoes.

See photograph page 48A.

note: This same idea could be used for other casseroles or leftover casseroles - for example, chili soup from chili con carne.

basic cream of vegetable soup ∅

yield: 4-5 cups (1-1.25 L) of soup

— *you choose your own favorite vegetable or combination of vegetables and then carry on with the recipe!*

3 cups	fresh OR frozen vegetables	
1 cup	chicken OR beef broth	750 mL
3 tbsp.	butter	250 mL
¼ cup	flour	45 mL
1 cup	milk	50 mL
1		250 mL
	egg, beaten (optional)	
1 cup	half & half (cereal cream) OR milk	1
	salt and pepper, to taste	250 mL

Combine vegetables with broth, bring to a boil, reduce heat, cover and simmer until vegetables are tender, 20-30 minutes depending on whether vegetables are frozen or fresh. Melt butter in a saucepan. Add flour to butter. Add milk gradually to flour and butter mixture (called roux). Combine egg and half & half, pour gradually into milk mixture, stirring constantly. Season with salt and pepper and any favorite spice (see spices, page 10). Cook over medium low heat - watch carefully or it will burn. DO NOT BOIL.

note: Some chopped onion and celery leaves, added to vegetables, will enhance the flavor of any soup.

variations:

1. Swiss or Cheddar cheese may be added.
2. Your vegetables (drained) may be pureéd in a blender, when cooked, but save the broth and add to the soup.

You can always know a real friend —
when you have made a fool of yourself
and he doesn't think you have done a permanent job!
Laurence J. Peter.

sauces

basic white sauce

— no-fail, no-fuss, no lumping!

thin:

1 tbsp.	butter OR margarine	15 mL
1 tbsp.	flour	15 mL
½ tsp.	salt	2 mL
dash	pepper	dash
1 cup	milk	250 mL

medium: use 2 tbsp. (30 mL) butter and flour for 1 cup (250 mL) of milk.

thick: use 3-4 tbsp. (45-60 mL) butter and flour for 1 cup (250 mL) of milk.

Melt butter in a pot or skillet (a heavy one if you have it). Add flour and seasonings. Stir to a smooth paste (roux). Add milk gradually, cook and stir sauce constantly until it is smooth and thick. If you have to keep it hot for any length of time, set your pot into a larger pot that has a bit of water in it, turn stove on low.

variations:

1. *cheese sauce* — add 1½ cups (375 mL) grated old cheese, ½ tsp. (2 mL) dry mustard and maybe even a dash of Worcestershire sauce to your medium white sauce. Great on broccoli, cauliflower, fish., etc.

2. *herb sauce* — add a few morsels of your favorite herbs - dill, basil, parsley, etc. to basic white sauce recipe.

3. *mornay sauce* — you need: 1 recipe basic white sauce - medium
   1 egg yolk
   2 tbsp. (30 mL) cream
   2 tbsp. (30 mL) Parmesan cheese
   ¼ cup (50 mL) grated Gruyère cheese

   Mix egg yolk and cream, with a bit of hot sauce, then return all to your basic sauce, stirring well. Stir in cheese until melted.

4. *easiest cream sauce* — dilute a 10 oz. (284 mL) can of cream soup (mushroom, celery, chicken, etc.) with about ½ cup (125 mL) of water, broth or milk (don't tell!).

vegetables

about vegetables

storage hints - for crispy, crunchy veggies!

— wash and core lettuce, run cold water into core hole, drain, put in a plastic bag and store in crisper.
— remove tops from carrots and radishes before refrigeration.
— trim off celery above the large stalks and store in separate plastic bag for use in soups, salads, etc. Rinse remainder under cold water and store in a plastic bag.
— trim off the leaves and stalk of cauliflower (some stalk can usually be trimmed and eaten raw or chopped and cooked with the florets).
— the tough stems on broccoli can be separated from the florets - the stems can then be peeled and eaten raw or cooked.
— green onions should be trimmed and bottom ends cut off.
— parsley can be washed. It stores well in a tightly covered jar in the refrigerator.
— "BEWARE" - trimmings from broccoli and cauliflower become "smelly" in the garbage even when put in plastic bags and, while we're on that subject, watch out for spoiled potatoes!
— for crunchy raw vegetables - store in the refrigerator in containers of cold water, but don't forget to change the water occasionally!

about onions

— you will shed fewer tears if you peel them under running water.
— to make slicing easier, cut the onion in half vertically, put the flat side on your cutting board and slice each half (if you insist on whole onion rings, you will have to do it the normal way!).

boiling:

— to boil most vegetables, bring water in pot to a boil, add a pinch of salt, toss in vegetables. (Use just enough water to barely cover the vegetables). Cover. When water has returned to a boil, turn heat down to a gentle boil and cook until just tender. Drain, season and butter. Serve as soon as possible.

stir-fry:

— clean and prepare vegetables, i.e. chop or julienne (cut in small strips); trim strings from pea pods, etc.
— heat a small amount of oil in a wok or frying pan, add quick-cooking vegetables such as pea pods (see photograph, page 32A), cherry tomatoes, mushrooms, celery and stir fry 2-3 minutes. Season to taste. (I prefer to do each vegetable individually).
— to stir-fry vegetables such as broccoli, turnip, cauliflower, carrots - stir fry in oil as above, add a bit of water, cover and steam just until tender. Drain if necessary. Season to taste with seasoning salt and pepper and maybe a wee bit of soy sauce.

creamed vegetables:

— please see directions for cream sauces, page 25.

creamed vegetables with a gourmet touch:

— simply sauté ¼ cup (50 mL) finely chopped celery in 2 tbsp. (30 mL) butter. Add ½ cup (125 mL) sour cream, ¼ cup (50 mL) dry white wine, 2 tbsp. (30 mL) parsley and a 10 oz. (284 mL) can cream of chicken soup (or another cream soup of your choice) to 2 cups (500 mL) cooked vegetables.

People can be divided into 3 groups:
— those who make things happen
— those who watch things happen
— those who wonder what happened!

plain ordinary baked potato

yield: 1 serving

Preheat oven 375°F (190°C)

— scrub potato thoroughly.
— prick with a fork (if you don't you'll be sorry when it explodes!).
— bake at 350°-400°F (180°-200°C) for about 1 hour. May also be brushed with oil or bacon fat and wrapped in foil for a more tender, palatable skin to munch on. If you want a crispy skin, don't wrap potato in foil.
— to serve: slit top of potato across in both directions and gently squeeze potato, with your fingers, to puff up. Top with sour cream, bacon bits, and/or chopped green onion.

note: Inserting metal skewers into the potato will speed up the baking time!

baked stuffed potato ∅

yield: 6-8 servings

— *simply delicious!*

Preheat oven 375°F (190°C)

4	baking potatoes	4
½ cup	cottage cheese	125 mL
¼ cup	butter	50 mL
1 tsp.	seasoning salt	5 mL
dash	pepper	dash
1-2 tbsp.	milk, warmed	15-30 mL
	grated Cheddar cheese	

Bake potatoes and cut in half lengthwise, or leave whole and slice off an oval shape on top. Gently scoop out inside, mash it and combine it with the remaining ingredients, except Cheddar cheese. Refill potato shells. Top with grated Cheddar cheese and reheat in your oven or on the barbecue.

variation:

1. Gently stir in ½ cup (125 mL) of cooked, chopped spinach or a wee bit of pimiento plus ⅓ cup (75 mL) Parmesan cheese and top with bacon bits.
2. May also be topped with sour cream.

See photograph page 80A.

potato casserole ∅

yield: 8-10 servings

Preheat oven 350°F (180°C)

— just great for company as it is prepared in advance.

6	large potatoes	6
2 cups	sour cream	500 mL
4-5	green onions, chopped	4-5
1½ cups	grated Cheddar cheese	375 mL
1½ tsp.	salt	7 mL
¼ tsp.	black pepper	1 mL
	paprika	

Bake or boil potatoes in their jackets (skins). Peel, shred on grater (messy, but worth it!). Stir remaining ingredients into potatoes, reserving ½ cup (125 mL) of cheese. Place mixture in a greased 13 x 9" (33 x 22cm) casserole. Cover, refrigerate overnight, or for several hours. Bake, uncovered, 30-40 minutes at 350°F (180°C) until hot and sizzly. Stir once during baking, then top with remaining cheese and paprika and finish baking.

parmesan potatoes ∅

yield: serves 6-8 healthy appetites!

Preheat oven 375°F (190°C)

— potatoes with pizzazz!

8	medium potatoes, unpeeled	8
½ cup	vegetable oil	125 mL
2 tbsp.	Parmesan cheese	30 mL
1 tsp.	salt	5 mL
¼ tsp.	black pepper	1 mL
½ tsp.	garlic salt	2 mL
½ tsp.	paprika	2 mL

Scrub potatoes and cut each into 4 lengthwise wedges. Arrange in a greased shallow pan. Mix all remaining ingredients and brush over potatoes. Place in oven and bake about 45 minutes or until golden brown and tender. Baste with pan drippings while baking.

scalloped potatoes ∅

yield: 6 servings

Preheat oven 350°F (180°C)

— *don't forget to grease the casserole for easy cleaning.*

4 cups	thinly sliced potatoes	
1½ cups	thinly sliced onions	1 L
2 tbsp.	flour	375 mL
	salt and pepper, to taste	30 mL
4 tbsp.	butter	
1¼ cups	milk, heated	60 mL
	paprika	300 mL

In a deep greased 2 quart (2 L) casserole, layer the potatoes, onions, flour, salt and pepper (about 3 layers of each). Dot with butter and pour milk over all. Sprinkle with paprika. Bake for about 1 hour or until tender.

note: — If you use a shallow casserole or want to make half the recipe, you may have to increase the amount of milk. The milk should just peek through the top layer.
— may be covered for 30-45 minutes, to speed up the cooking.

variation:

Omit the flour, butter and milk and use either a 10 oz. (284 mL) can consommé, undiluted, or a 10 oz. (284 mL) can mushroom soup diluted with 5 oz. (142 mL) milk.

oven-crisp potatoes

yield: allow 1 good-sized potato per serving   *Preheat oven 400°F (200°C)*

— *a big favorite in our family!*

> potatoes
> margarine OR butter
> seasoning salt

Put layers of thinly sliced, peeled (or unpeeled) potatoes into a greased shallow casserole with bits of margarine or butter between layers. Season the layers with seasoning salt.

Bake, covered, 30 minutes at 400°F (200°C). Uncover and bake until slightly browned.

note: Layers of thinly sliced onion are good in this recipe. Can also be put in a packet of foil and done on the barbecue - but don't forget to grease the foil!

spanish rice Ø

yield: 6-8 servings

Preheat oven 350°F (180°C)

—just add hot crusty rolls and a green salad and dinner is ready!

6 slices	bacon	6 slices
1 cup	long-grain rice, uncooked	250 mL
1	onion, sliced	1
1	medium green pepper, chopped	1
28 oz.	can tomatoes, chopped	796 mL
1 tsp.	salt	5 mL
2 tsp.	paprika	10 mL
1	garlic clove, minced	1

Fry bacon until crisp, remove from pan and crumble. Lightly brown rice in bacon fat in frying pan. Remove to greased 6-cup (1.5 L) casserole. Sauté onion and pepper in bacon fat and add to casserole. Add tomatoes, seasoning and bacon. Cover, bake 45-60 minutes or until the rice is tender.

note: — This recipe could also be simmered over low heat in a heavy skillet (covered) instead of the oven method.
— Use 14 oz. (398 mL) can of tomatoes if halving recipe.

chinese fried rice Ø

yield: 6-8 servings

½ cup	ham, chicken, pork OR bacon, diced	125 mL
2 tbsp.	vegetable oil	30 mL
10 oz.	can sliced mushrooms, drained OR ½ cup (125 mL) fresh, sliced mushrooms	284 mL
3	chopped green onions	3
½ cup	red OR green pepper, chopped	125 mL
4 cups	cooked rice	1 L
2-3 tbsp.	soy sauce	30-45 mL
1 tbsp.	butter	15 mL
1	egg, well beaten	1

Fry meat lightly in oil. Set meat aside. Sauté vegetables for 2-3 minutes. Add rice, soy sauce and cooked meat to the vegetables in frying pan. Cook over low heat, about 5-10 minutes, stirring often. Push all ingredients to one side, melt butter and scramble the egg in butter. Mix all together and serve.

See photograph page 32A.

wild rice casserole

yield: 6-8 servings

Preheat oven 350°F (180°C)

6 oz.	pkg. Uncle Ben's Wild Rice Mix	170 g
1 cup	cooked Minute Rice	250 mL
1 cup	chopped onion	250 mL
1 cup	chopped celery	250 mL
3 tbsp.	butter OR margarine	45 mL
¼ cup	soy sauce	50 mL
10 oz.	can mushrooms, drained, sliced	284 mL
3 oz.	can water chestnuts, drained, sliced	94 mL
⅓ cup	slivered almonds	75 mL

Prepare rice as directed on package. Add remaining ingredients, except almonds. Place in a 2-quart (2 L) greased casserole. Sprinkle top with almonds. Bake, covered, ½ hour or until hot.

note: Feel free to leave out the mushrooms, water chestnuts or almonds. If you don't like rice - forget the whole thing!

test prayer

Now I lay me down to study,
I pray the Lord I won't go nutty,
If I should fail to learn this junk,
I pray the Lord I will not flunk.
But if I do, don't pity me at all,
Just lay my bones down in the study hall.
Tell my teacher I did my best,
Then pile my books upon my chest,
Now I lay me down to rest
And pray I'll pass tomorrow's test.
If I should die before I wake,
That's one less test I'll have to take.

Sufferin Student

chinese dinner — easy and delicious

vegetable frittata Ø

yield: 8 servings

Preheat oven 350°F (180°C)

— a frittata is similar to a quiche, but easier because there is no crust. This particular one features artichoke so you will probably want to pass it by - DON'T - either brave the artichokes or substitute broccoli, mushrooms, etc. This is a very tasty, colourful and versatile dish!

3 tbsp.	butter	45 mL
1	onion, finely chopped	1
1	garlic clove, minced	1
1	green pepper, diced	1
½	red pepper, diced (optional)	½
¼ cup	chopped parsley	50 mL
2 x 6 oz.	jar marinated artichokes, drained, diced	2 x 170 mL
5	eggs	5
½ cup	soft bread crumbs	125 mL
1 tsp.	salt	5 mL
¼ tsp.	pepper	1 mL
¼ tsp.	Tabasco sauce	1 mL
1 tsp.	Worcestershire sauce	5 mL
2 cups	grated Swiss cheese	500 mL

In a frying pan, sauté onion and garlic in butter. Add peppers and cook 5 minutes longer. Add parsley and diced artichokes. Remove from heat.

Beat eggs and add remaining ingredients. Stir in vegetables. Put mixture in a greased 9 x 9 x 2" (22 x 22 x 5 cm) round or square pan, 6-cup (1.5 L) capacity. Bake for 30 minutes or until golden.

note: — For half recipe use 3 eggs.
 — May be prepared ahead of time and baked just before serving.

variation:
Feeling creative? Try a different cheese.

To handle yourself - use your head. To handle others - use your heart.

potato salad Ø

yield: 12 servings

— always a favorite — enjoyed by all!

6	large potatoes	
4	hard-boiled eggs (see below)	6
2	celery stalks with leaves, chopped	4
1	tomato, chopped	2
3	green onions, chopped	1
¾-1 cup	mayonnaise	3
1 tsp.	seasoning salt	175-250 mL
½ tsp.	pepper	5 mL
¾ tsp.	dry mustard	2 mL
	paprika (optional)	7 mL

Peel and boil potatoes just until tender. Drain, cool and chop into bite-sized pieces. Chop eggs (reserving 1 to decorate the top if you wish) add to potatoes.

Mix mayonnaise with seasonings and add to potato mixture. Sprinkle with paprika.

note: — Potato salad is best if made a few hours ahead to allow the flavors to blend.
— REMINDER - potato salad should always be refrigerated before serving and leftovers returned to the refrigerator as soon as possible. Potato salad that is more than a day old should be tossed out - and if you take it on a picnic, don't bring it back!

helpful hints: — Always wipe off the top of mayonnaise jars if they look grungy.
— To hard boil eggs, put your eggs in a saucepan, cover with cold water. Bring water to a boil then simmer 10-15 minutes. Drain and cover with cold water to prevent discoloration of the yolk!

caesar salad Ø

yield: 6-8 servings

— *there are so many recipes for this salad - I hope you enjoy this one - if not, just adjust to your own taste. My family always complains of not enough garlic and if they knew I put anchovies into it, I'd be in deep trouble!*

2	large garlic cloves, minced	2
2 cups	bread cubes	500 mL
2 tbsp.	vegetable oil	30 mL
1	large head romaine lettuce, 10-12 cups (2.5-3 L)	1
2	large garlic cloves, minced	2
½ cup	vegetable oil (olive oil preferred)	125 mL
2 tbsp.	lemon juice	30 mL
2	egg yolks	2
1½ tsp.	Worcestershire sauce	7 mL
½ tsp.	dry mustard	2 mL
½ tsp.	freshly ground black pepper	2 mL
3	anchovies, drained, finely chopped	3
¾ tsp.	salt	3 mL
½ cup	freshly grated Parmesan cheese	125 mL

Combine first 3 ingredients, toss all together and bake at 350°F (180°C) for 10-15 minutes. Watch carefully and stir a couple of times.

Wash the lettuce and drain well, then place in a plastic bag and refrigerate.

Combine the remaining ingredients, using ¼ cup (50 mL) of the Parmesan cheese, in a jar and shake well to mix. Refrigerate.

Just before serving, tear lettuce into bite-size pieces. Toss with enough dressing to coat thoroughly. Add remaining ¼ cup (50 mL) Parmesan cheese and croutons and toss again.

note: I freeze the remaining anchovies for use another time.

variations:
1. A bit of wine vinegar may be added.
2. Dijon mustard may be substituted for the dry mustard.

did you know? — Olive oil is stored at room temperature!

secrets to success — Soak garlic in oil 24 hrs. before making dressing.
— To keep lettuce crisp, add dressing just before serving.

spinach salad Ø

yield: 6-8 servings

— a nutritious meal in itself!

1-2	bunches spinach	
1 cup	sliced mushrooms	1-2
3	hard-boiled eggs, chopped (see page 34)	250 mL
		3
5	bacon slices, cooked crisp	
½	red onion, thinly sliced OR 3 green onions, chopped	5
		½

Wash and dry spinach - store in plastic bag in refrigerator until needed.

Just before serving, tear spinach into bite-sized pieces and toss together with other ingredients. Serve with lemon-mustard dressing below.

variation:

1. Add ½ cup (125 mL) shredded Swiss cheese.
2. Use chopped egg white in salad and mashed egg yolk for garnish.

See photograph page 48A.

lemon-mustard dressing

2 tbsp.	lemon juice	30 mL
½ tsp.	dry mustard	2 mL
2 tbsp.	sugar	30 mL
1	garlic clove, crushed (optional)	1
½ tsp.	salt	2 mL
dash	freshly ground black pepper	dash
½ cup	vegetable oil	125 mL

Mix all together - adding oil at the last. To blend dressing ingredients well, put them in a jar and shake vigorously. Refrigerate until serving time.

tahitian fruit salad with lime dressing Ø

yield: 15-20 servings

Do try it - it may well become a favorite!

1	large pineapple	1
1	large papaya	1
1	large cantelope	1
2	cans mandarin oranges, well drained	2
2 cups	fresh strawberries	500 mL
1	large banana, sliced	1

Cut pineapple, papaya and cantelope into bite-size chunks. Add oranges and marinate fruit in lime dressing, see recipe below. Chill 1-2 hours, stirring occasionally. Add strawberries and banana just before serving. This makes a large salad but quantity is easily adjusted to suit your needs.

lime dressing

2 tbsp.	fresh lime juice	30 mL
¼ cup	light rum	50 mL
⅓ cup	honey	75 mL
1 tsp.	grated lime peel	5 mL

Combine all ingredients well.

*You can fool all of the people some of the time,
and some of the people all of the time
but you can't fool MOM.*

oil and lemon dressing

1	garlic clove, minced	1
1 tsp.	salt	5 mL
¼ tsp.	black pepper	1 mL
3-4 tbsp.	lemon juice	45-60 mL
¼ cup	vegetable oil	50 mL

Combine all ingredients and mix well.

"house" salad dressing

yields: 6-8 servings

— *just as most fancy restaurants feature "house" wines, I like to surprise dinner guests by passing our favorite "house" salad dressing for tossed salads!*

2 tsp.	salt	10 mL
½ tsp.	freshly ground black pepper	2 mL
2 tsp.	sugar	10 mL
½ tsp.	dry mustard	2 mL
1 tsp.	celery seed	5 mL
½ cup	mayonnaise	125 mL
2 tbsp.	red wine vinegar	30 mL
¼ cup	olive oil	50 mL

Combine all ingredients in blender until smooth (or put in jar and shake vigorously).

note: The amounts of wine vinegar and oil may be varied to suit your taste.

Love is like the five loaves and two fishes. It doesn't start to multiply until you give it away.

whole-wheat muffins

yield: 12 large muffins

preheat oven 375°F (180°C)

— for munching at breakfast, lunch or for midnight snacks!

1 cup	chopped dates	250 mL
1 tsp.	baking soda	5 mL
¾ cup	boiling water	175 mL
1	egg	1
¾ cup	brown sugar	175 mL
1 tsp.	salt	5 mL
1 tsp.	vanilla	5 mL
1 tsp.	baking powder	5 mL
1½ cups	whole-wheat flour*	375 mL
½ cup	chopped walnuts (optional)	125 mL
¼ cup	melted butter	50 mL

Combine dates and soda. Pour boiling water over date mixture. Let cool.

Beat the egg in a mixing bowl. Add brown sugar, salt and vanilla and then stir in date mixture.

Mix baking powder and whole-wheat flour and add to batter. Stir in walnuts. Add melted butter and stir until blended.

Fill muffin cups ⅔ full and bake at 375°F (190°C) for 15-20 minutes.

* You can substitute 1 cup (250 mL) whole-wheat flour plus ½ cup (125 mL) wheat germ.

Don't forget the melted butter (as I almost have occasionally)!

See photograph page 96A.

date muffins

yield: 12 muffins

preheat oven 350°F (180°C)

— *originally called "dipsy doodlers" because they are dipped in candy glaze.*

½ cup	boiling water	
½ tsp.	baking soda	125 mL
1 cup	chopped dates	2 mL
¼ cup	soft margarine	250 mL
¾ cup	brown sugar	50 mL
1	egg	175 mL
1 tsp.	vanilla	1
1½ cups	flour	5 mL
1 tsp.	baking powder	375 mL
¼ tsp.	salt	5 mL
½ cup	mashed banana	1 mL
¼ cup	chopped nuts (optional)	125 mL
		50 mL

Pour boiling water over dates and baking soda. Set aside.

Cream together margarine and sugar. Beat in egg and vanilla.

Mix dry ingredients together and add to egg mixture. Stir in banana and nuts and finally add date mixture. Stir just until blended.

Fill muffins cups ⅔ full and bake 20-25 minutes. Dip tops in warm glaze, see recipe below.

glaze:

¼ cup	brown sugar	
2 tbsp.	butter	50 mL
2 tbsp.	milk	30 mL
		30 mL

Combine all ingredients and heat until sugar is dissolved.

note: The glaze is optional of course, but does add a delicious touch and makes them a wee bit different from most muffins.

See photograph page 96A.

boiled raisin cupcakes

yield: 12 cupcakes

preheat oven 350°F (180°C)

— very tasty morsels with their own unique flavor.

1½ cups	raisins (rinsed in water & drained)	375 mL
¼ cup	margarine	50 mL
½ cup	white sugar	125 mL
¼ cup	brown sugar	50 mL
1	egg, slightly beaten	1
¼ tsp.	salt	1 mL
1½ cups	flour	375 mL
1 tsp.	baking soda	5 mL
1 tsp.	cinnamon	5 mL
½ tsp.	cloves	2 mL
½ tsp.	nutmeg	2 mL
½ cup	raisin water	125 mL

Put washed raisins in a pot, cover with water. Simmer 20 minutes. Strain, RESERVING ½ cup (125 mL) raisin water.

Cream margarine and sugars. Add the beaten egg.

Mix dry ingredients together and add alternately with raisin water to creamed mixture. Fold in raisins.

Fill greased muffin tins about ⅔ full and bake about 20 minutes.

See photograph page 96A.

IF U FIND MISLAKES---in this publication, pleese Consider that they r there four a purpose. Wee publish some thing four everyone, and som peoplE r alvays loking for MISTALES!!!

breads

cinnamon buns Ø

yield: 18-20 buns

preheat oven 375°F (190°C)

— take the easy way out with this recipe!

2 loaves	frozen bread dough	
¾ cup	brown sugar	2 loaves
3 tbsp.	butter	175 mL
1½ tbsp.	corn syrup	45 mL
3 tbsp.	cold water	22 mL
	butter OR margarine, brown sugar & cinnamon for spreading on dough	45 mL

Put frozen dough in large bowl, cover and allow to rise until doubled in volume (if you push a finger into the dough and the indentation remains, dough is ready). Boil the brown sugar, butter, syrup and cold water for only 3 or 4 minutes and pour into a 13 x 9" (33 x 22 cm) pan. When your dough has risen, punch down gently and roll out on lightly floured board to ¼" (.6 cm) thick, shaping into a rectangle about 14 x 18" (35 x 45 cm). Spread with softened butter, a layer of brown sugar and a liberal amount of cinnamon, I use about 2-3 tsp. (10-15 mL). Now, roll up jelly-roll fashion, sealing edges by pinching together. Cut into 1" (2.5 cm) thickness and set on top of syrup in pan. Once again allow to rise until doubled. Bake at 375°F (190°C) for 20-25 minutes. Allow to rest in pan for 5 minutes, then turn upside down onto a cookie sheet.

note: — These are the sticky "finger-lickin' good" variety of cinnamon buns.
— If you prefer, you could use only half the syrup mixture - or none at all!

hints: — Try thawing the dough overnight in the refrigerator if you want to make these early on the next day.
— If you happen to have a microwave oven, the dough thaws beautifully on defrost in 5-10 minutes.

cheese circle bread

preheat oven 400°F (200°C)

— *a thick layer of yummy melted cheese baked between 2 layers of bread dough - a tasty complement for any menu.*

1	frozen bread loaf	1
1	egg, beaten	1
3 cups	shredded Muenster cheese	750 mL
½ cup	snipped parsley	125 mL
½ tsp.	garlic salt	2 mL
⅛ tsp.	black pepper	0.5 mL
1	egg, slightly beaten	1
1 tbsp.	water	15 mL
2 tsp.	sesame seeds (optional)	10 mL

Defrost bread and allow to rise until double. Punch down and divide in half. Roll out 1 portion to fit a 12" (30 cm) pizza pan.

Combine beaten egg with cheese, parsley, garlic and pepper and spread on dough.

Roll out second portion of dough and put on top of mixture. Seal the edges by pinching with fingers (as for double pie crust). Make a few ½" (1.3 cm) slits in top crust. Allow to sit, covered, 30-60 minutes.

Bake in 400°F (200°C) oven for 20 minutes until light brown. Remove from oven and brush top with egg and water mixed. Sprinkle with sesame seeds, if desired. Return to oven and bake an additional 5-10 minutes.

Serve hot, cutting into narrow wedges.

Happiness is like jam - it is hard to spread even a little without getting some on yourself.

43

french toast

yield: 1 serving

— a great way to start the day!

1	egg	
2 tbsp.	milk	1
drop	vanilla	30 mL
pinch	salt	drop
2 tbsp.	butter	pinch
	thick slices of day-old French bread*	30 mL

Beat together egg, milk, vanilla and salt. Preheat frying pan and add the butter. Dip bread in egg mixture for about 10 seconds, coating both sides. Brown bread in frying pan, on both sides. Serve with butter and syrup or your favorite jam.

*slices of ordinary bread will do fine!

note: These may be dusted with icing sugar.

feather-light hot cakes Ø

yield: 8-10 pancakes

— you're in for a real treat with these pancakes!

1	egg, beaten	
1 cup	milk	1
2 tbsp.	vegetable oil	250 mL
1 cup	flour	30 mL
½ tsp.	salt	250 mL
2 tbsp.	baking powder*	2 mL
2 tbsp.	sugar	30 mL
		30 mL

Combine all ingredients and beat just until smooth.

Bake on a hot greased griddle.

* I'm not kidding - use 2 tbsp. (30 mL)

note: — To test griddle for correct heat, sprinkle a few drops of water on the surface - drops should bounce around when the "correct" temperature is reached.

— You can still use whole egg if halving recipe.

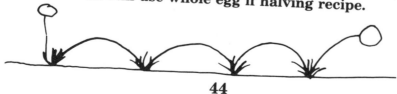

western sandwich Ø

yield: 3-4 servings

— quick and easy for when you are in a big hurry!

¼ cup	chopped onion	50 mL
¼ cup	chopped green pepper	50 mL
2 tbsp.	chopped celery	30 mL
2 tbsp.	butter	30 mL
½ cup	chopped ham OR bacon	125 mL
4	eggs	4
¼ cup	milk	50 mL
	salt and pepper, to taste	
	toast OR buns, split & toasted	

Sauté vegetables in butter for 2-3 minutes. Add ham. Beat eggs and milk lightly. Add salt and pepper. Pour egg mixture into vegetables in skillet. Cook just until set, using medium heat. Cut into 4 wedges and flip each over. Serve on toast or buns with ketchup or chili sauce.

note: Mushrooms could be added too!

Smiling is happy, fun, feels good, looks nice and doesn't cost anything.

monte cristo sandwich Ø

yield: 2 servings

— serve with soup and salad for a very satisfying meal!

4 slices	bread	4 slices
	butter OR margarine	
	hot mustard	
2 slices	ham (leftover baked ham is great)	2 slices
2 slices	mozzarella cheese	2 slices
1	egg	1
2 tbsp.	milk OR cream	30 mL
dash	salt	dash

Spread bread with butter and hot mustard and top with 1 slice each of ham and cheese and another slice of bread. Repeat above steps with remaining bread, ham and cheese. Beat egg, milk and salt in shallow dish and dip sandwich (both sides) in mixture.

In frying pan, over medium heat, add a bit of butter and brown each sandwich on both sides.

May be served with ketchup or jelly.

See photograph page 48A.

reuben sandwich

yield: 1 serving

— a classic favorite!

2 slices	rye bread	2 slices
1 tbsp.	Thousand Island Dressing (optional)	15 mL
1 slice	Swiss cheese	1 slice
2 tbsp.	sauerkraut, drained	30 mL
2 oz.	corned beef	55 g
	butter	

Layer a slice of bread with dressing, cheese, sauerkraut and corned beef. Top with second bread slice. Butter bread on outside, both sides. In a frying pan, over medium heat, add a bit of butter and brown sandwich on both sides.

Serve with dill pickles.

tuna-cheese snack Ø

yield: 2-4 servings

6.5 oz.	can tuna OR salmon, crab, etc.	184 g
½ cup	grated old Cheddar cheese OR other cheese of your choice	125 mL
4 tbsp.	mayonnaise	60 mL
1 tsp.	chopped onion	5 mL
1 tsp.	horseradish	5 mL
	French bread or split buns	

Combine all ingredients and spread on slices of French bread. Broil until brown.

note: When halving recipe, use a 3.3 oz. (94 mL) can of fish.

fried egg sandwich

yield: 1 serving

1 tbsp.	butter	15 mL
1 tsp.	chopped onion	5 mL
1	egg	1
2 slices	buttered bread OR toast	2 slices

In a frying pan, melt butter and sauté onion. Add egg, bread yolk and scramble slightly. When set, flip over. Serve between slices of bread or toast.

variation:
Using a kaiser or hamburger bun, spread with hot mustard, slip in a slice of ham or back bacon, some fried onion slices and a fried egg (directions given above). The men love these!

There is no sense in advertising your troubles. There is no market for them.

poached egg

yield: 1 serving

	butter	
	water	
	salt, to taste	
1	egg	1
1	slice of toast	1

Grease bottom of saucepan. Fill with water to twice depth of egg. Add salt. Bring water to boil. Break egg and drop gently into water. Simmer until egg white is firm. Remove with slotted spoon. Drain well. Serve on toast.

note: 1 tsp. (5 mL) vinegar added to water helps egg to retain perfect shape.

variation:
May be topped with mornay sauce, page 25.

ALAN ALDA said, "Be bold when you embark for strange places don't leave any of yourself safely on shore. Have the nerve to go into unexplored territory. Be brave enough to live life creatively. The creative is the place where no one else has been. You have to leave the city of your comfort and go into the wilderness of your intuition. You can't get there by bus, only hard work and risk and by not quite knowing what you're doing. What you'll discover is wonderful. What you'll discover is yourself".

the best lunch in town

let's talk meat!

amounts to purchase:

1 lb. (500 g) boneless meat — 4 servings

1 lb. (500 g) meat with small amount of bone — 3 servings

1 lb. (500 g) meat with large amount of bone (e.g. spareribs) — 2 servings

approximate cooking guide for meats

turkey - 10-16 lbs. (5-8 kg)	325°F (160°C)	25-30 min./lb.(500 g)
ham - precooked	325°F (160°C)	15-20 min./lb.(500 g)
- not precooked	325°F (160°C)	20-25 min./lb.(500 g)
fresh pork	350°F (180°C)	30-40 min./lb.(500 g)
roast beef	325°F (160°C)	25-35 min./lb.(500 g)

There are so many variables when it comes to roasting meats that it is virtually impossible to provide an accurate guide for roasting. The size of your roast (large roasts take fewer minutes/lb. [kg]), the quality, the amount of bone (the larger amount of bone, the fewer minutes/lb. [kg] are required) - also the type of pan, the temperature of the roast when put in the oven as well as degree of doneness desired, all are factors which determine the cooking times.

Meat thermometers are invaluable (just be sure to position them so they are not resting on the bone).

Allow roasts to stand (covered) 15-20 minutes before carving, if possible. Carve against the grain of the meat.

When in doubt, strike up an acquaintance with your butcher. They usually enjoy sharing their knowledge and expertise.

beef

pot roast # 1

— easiest on the budget - includes hip and rump cuts - just beware of too much bone.

Wipe roast clean and season with salt, pepper, garlic, salt or pepper, etc. Place in a heavy pot and brown, on top of the stove, on all sides using 2-3 tbsp. (30-45 mL) oil. Remove from heat and add liquid (enough to cover about ⅓ of the roast). Put in 300°F (150°C) oven and simmer about 3 hours for a roast weighing 4-6 lbs. (2-3 kg).

For liquid, you may use beef broth, packaged onion soup mix, (mixed with water), canned tomatoes or tomato juice, etc.

Add washed, peeled and cut-up vegetables during the last hour of cooking - potatoes, carrots, turnips, onions, celery, etc.

Before serving, if you wish to make gravy out of the cooking liquid: Remove meat from pan, cover. Drain off excess fat. Mix about 4 tbsp. (60 mL) flour and 1 tsp (5 mL) sugar with ½ cup (125 mL) cold water in a jar and shake vigorously. Gradually stir this into the hot liquid. Stir and cook until thick.

note: — You probably will not need all the flour mix.
— If lumps persist, strain when no one is looking!

pot roast #2

Take a large piece of foil and double it. Place your meat in the middle of the foil. Top with a 10 oz. (284 mL) can of mushroom soup plus ½ package of onion soup mix, (dry). Fold foil securely with double folds. Put meat in roasting pan. Bake at 300°F (150°C) for about 3 hours.

Presto! Beef and gravy all in one (and thickened for you)!

conventional roasts

— standing rib, cross-rib, etc.

Place roast in a shallow pan, preferably on a rack. Season with salt, pepper, garlic, etc. (some cooks save the salt until the last for a juicier roast). Bake at 325°F (160°C) until desired degree of doneness. See roasting guide page 49.

note: Always wipe off meats with a damp cloth and pat dry - please!

good gravy

— with secrets for the best-tasting gravy with NO lumps!

Remove roast, turkey, etc. from roasting pan. Cover meat to keep warm.

Skim off excess fat (not the meat drippings, just the fat!).

Place your roasting pan over medium heat on the stove.

Blend in flour - approximately 2 tbsp. (30 mL) flour for 1 tbsp. (15 mL) fat to make 1 cup (250 mL) of gravy. A small roast will usually allow for 1 cup (250 mL) of gravy. Stir just until browned.

Now you can add your liquid gradually - you may use beef or chicken broth, milk, potato water, etc. or just plain water. Keep stirring until thickened and lumps have disappeared.

Check seasoning.

hints: — A few chopped onions may be simmered in the drippings before adding your flour.
— Kitchen bouquet, steak sauce or even ketchup may be added for flavor.
— If your gravy is too thin, mix some flour and cold water with a wee bit of sugar in a jar. Shake well - add gradually to gravy while boiling.

note: If your roast is very small you may only have a few brown drippings in your pan and not enough for good gravy so forget it!

yorkshire pudding

yield: 10-12 servings

— *many excellent cooks shy away from making these but my intuition tells me that you can handle it. (WARNING - my intuition is not always right!) Anyway, your dinner will not be ruined if they fail. The worst that could happen would possibly be a bruised ego!*

first — Plan to have your roast cooked 40 minutes ahead so that your oven can be turned to 425°F (220°C). Cover roast to keep warm.

second — Beat together with an electric mixer just until smooth:

1 cup	flour	250 mL
½ tsp.	salt	2 mL
1 cup	milk	250 mL
2	eggs	2

Refrigerate batter for about an hour if possible.

third — Preheat muffin tins in oven. Using the fat from your roast or vegetable oil put 1 tsp. (5 mL) in each muffin cup. Pour batter into each until barely ⅔ full.

fourth — Bake at 425°F (220°C) for 25-35 minutes. Serve as soon as possible.

hints: — Set the muffin pans on rimmed cookie sheets in case the fat runs over. (Sprinkle spills with salt for easy clean-up.)
— Use your deepest muffin tins.

Never put off until tomorrow what you can avoid altogether.

burgundy steak Ø

yield: 6-8 servings

— *this dish is almost a stir-fry variety, depending on the type of steak used. You can use flank or top round or sirloin if time is precious. If not, use the cross-rib, bottom round or blade varieties - whichever, the flavor is excellent.*

		500 g-1 kg
1-2 lb.	steak	45 mL
3 tbsp.	vegetable oil	500 mL
2 cups	sliced onions	250 mL
1 cup	sliced mushrooms	2
2	beef cubes (Oxo)	425 mL
1¾ cups	water	5 mL
1 tsp.	Worcestershire sauce	500 mL
2 cups	diced carrots	75 mL
⅓ cup	Burgundy OR dry red wine	500 mL
2 cups	sliced celery	30 mL
2 tbsp.	cornstarch	50 mL
¼ cup	water	

Slice meat (against the grain) into thin slices. Brown quickly in hot oil in large skillet. Remove meat from pan and set aside.

Brown onions and mushrooms in skillet.

Dissolve beef cube in water. Add beef broth, Worcestershire sauce, carrots and wine to skillet.

Return meat to skillet. Cover, simmer until tender (1-1½ hrs. for less tender cuts).

Add celery to mixture.

Mix cornstarch and water. Stir into skillet mixture and cook until thickened.

Relax and enjoy a scrumptious dinner - serve with a baked potato or noodles!

Definition of a big toe - a device for locating sharp objects in the dark.

pepper steak ∅

yield: 4-6 servings

— my husband's very favorite!

1	large onion, chopped	1
10 oz.	can sliced mushrooms OR 1 cup (250 mL) fresh	284 mL
3 tbsp.	vegetable oil	45 mL
1½ lbs.	round steak, thinly sliced	750 g
1	chicken bouillon cube	1
½ cup	hot water	125 mL
1	garlic clove, minced	1
3 tbsp.	soy sauce	45 mL
1 tbsp.	sugar	15 mL
¼ tsp.	pepper	1 mL
1	green pepper, sliced	1
1½ tsp.	cornstarch	7 mL
2 tbsp.	water	30 mL

In a skillet sauté onions and mushrooms in 1 tbsp. (15 mL) of oil. Remove from skillet and set aside.

Add remaining oil to skillet and brown meat quickly. Add chicken broth (bouillon cube dissolved in hot water) and garlic to meat and simmer, covered, until meat is tender, 30-45 minutes.

Add sautéed onions and mushrooms, soy sauce, sugar, pepper and green pepper. Simmer 10 minutes.

Mix cornstarch with water and add to meat mixture, stirring until thickened.

Serve on fluffy rice.

No amount of planning will ever replace dumb luck.

frying pan stew Ø
(Auntie Myrt's special recipe)

yield: 8 servings

— *if you like curry and sausage, this recipe is superb. The aroma of it cooking is guaranteed to start the gastric juices flowing!*

1½ lbs.	steak (round, flank, sirloin)	750 g
1½ lbs.	pork sausage	750 g
1	onion, sliced	1
	salt and pepper, to taste	
	water	500 mL
2 cups	raw macaroni	
	curry, to taste (we like Spice Island curry)	

Cut steak and sausage into bite-size pieces and brown well in large skillet. Add sliced onion, salt and pepper and enough water to barely cover the meat.

Cover and simmer until beef is tender (about 1 or 2 hours). If you use sirloin steak, cooking time is about ½ hour.

Reduce liquid almost entirely by uncovering pan and turning up the heat. Allow it to boil vigorously.

Meanwhile, cook macaroni as directed just until tender. Drain, rinse with cold water. Add macaroni and curry to taste - it should be fairly spicy.

note: — Cooking time varies in this recipe depending on the type of beef used, degree of tenderness desired and probably how hungry you are!
— Myrt leaves her sausages whole!

Backbone is better than wishbone.

beef stew Ø
(for the weekend)

yield 6-8 servings

Preheat oven 250°F (120°C)

— *if you ever find an easier stew, please send me the recipe!*

1½ lbs.	stewing beef *	750 g
19 oz.	can tomatoes OR tomato juice	540 mL
1	pkg. dry onion soup mix	1
2 tbsp.	sugar	30 mL
2 cups	chopped raw carrots, parsnips, turnips, celery, etc.	500 mL

Cut beef into bite-size pieces and put in 6-cup (1.5 L) casserole. (Do not brown.)

Add tomatoes, soup mix (you may only want to use ½ pkg.) and sugar. Simmer, covered, 3-4 hours.

Add vegetables to stew during last hour of cooking.

To thicken, just mix 2 tbsp. (30 mL) flour, plus ½ tsp. (2 mL) sugar with some cold water. (I usually do this in a jar, shake well and add what I need). Allow to cook until thickened.

Serve with hot rolls and salad.

note: The sugar prevents a lumpy gravy!

penny saver hint: — You will find it less expensive to buy a cheap roast or steak such as blade, chuck or cross rib, avoid excess bone and fat. Cut and trim your own stew meat.

a different kind of bone study

The body of almost every organization has "four" kinds of bones:
1. *The "Wishbones," who spend all their time wishing someone else would do all the work.*
2. *The "Jawbones," who do all the talking but little else.*
3. *The "Knucklebones," who knock everything that everyone else tries to do.*
4. *The "Backbones," who get under the workload and get things done.*

braised beef shortribs Ø

yield: 4-6 servings

Preheat oven 350°F (180°C)

— shortribs (bone-in variety) are actually one of the tastiest meats to cook.
   However, do watch for lean ribs - if you can only find fatty ones, save
   this recipe for another day!

2 tbsp.	chili powder	30 mL
1½ tsp.	salt	7 mL
½ tsp.	thyme (optional)	2 mL
2-3 lbs.	beef shortribs	1-1.5 kg
1	garlic clove, minced	1
1	large onion, thinly sliced	1
3 tbsp.	vegetable oil	45 mL
1½ cups	dry red wine, beer OR beef broth	375 mL

Combine chili, salt and thyme. Rub into meat, covering all surfaces.

Sauté garlic and onion in skillet and put into an 8-cup (2 L) casserole
or Dutch oven.

Brown ribs in skillet, using more oil if necessary. Add to casserole.
Add wine.

Bake for at least 2 hours until tender. These have a really zesty flavor
and are delicious served on a bed of noodles.

hint: — Cover your casserole with foil if you don't have a lid.
        — You may want to remove excess fat by soaking it off with
          a slice of bread or just by spooning it off.

*Anytime the going seems easy you had better check
and see if you are going downhill.*

beef stroganoff Ø

yield: 6-8 servings

3 slices	bacon, diced	3 slices
1½ lbs.	lean ground beef	750 g
½ cup	chopped onion	125 mL
1½ tbsp.	flour	22 mL
¾ tsp.	salt	3 mL
¼ tsp.	paprika	1 mL
dash	black pepper	dash
10 oz.	can cream of mushroom soup	284 mL
1 cup	sour cream	250 mL
8	hamburger buns	8

Pan-fry diced bacon. Remove from pan. Brown beef and onion in bacon fat. Drain off excess fat. Add bacon.

Blend together flour and seasonings. Add to meat and bacon. Add soup and cook 10-20 minutes.

Stir in sour cream and heat thoroughly. DO NOT BOIL.

Serve on toasted buns.

note: This is very rich and you may want to use only ½ cup (125 mL) of the sour cream.

mushroom burgers Ø

yield: 4 servings

1 lb.	ground beef	500 g
10 oz.	can mushroom soup	284 mL
⅔ cup	dry bread crumbs	150 mL
2 tbsp.	minced onion	30 mL
1 tbsp.	chopped parsley (optional)	15 mL
1	egg, slightly beaten	1
¼ cup	water	50 mL

Mix meat with ¼ can of soup, bread crumbs, onion, parsley and egg. Shape into patties. Brown in greased skillet.

Blend remaining soup with water. Pour over patties. Heat thoroughly.

Serve on toasted buns with a salad for a quick snack!

chili con carne

yield: 6-8 servings

— a great budget dish!

1½-2 lbs.	ground beef	750 g - 1 kg
1	medium onion, chopped	1
	salt and pepper, to taste	
dash	garlic powder (optional)	dash
	chopped green pepper (optional)	
	sliced mushrooms (optional)	
10 oz.	can tomato soup	284 mL
14 oz.	can kidney beans	398 mL
1 cup	water OR beef broth	250 mL
2-3 tbsp.	chili powder	30-45 mL

Brown beef and onion and season with salt and pepper. Add garlic, green pepper and mushrooms if desired. Add soup, beans and broth. Add chili powder gradually (to taste).

Simmer about 1 hour for best flavor, but, if in a hurry, you'll enjoy it the way it is!

chili dogs

yield: 1 serving

— a yummy combination!

Split hot dog bun lengthwise and toast under broiler (optional, of course). Top with hot dog, chili and chopped onion (if desired). A bit messy to eat, but worth it!

lasagne ∅

Preheat oven 350°F (180°C)

2 lbs.	ground beef	1 kg
2	garlic cloves, minced	2
1 tsp.	black pepper	5 mL
2 tsp.	seasoning salt	10 mL
28 oz.	can tomatoes	796 mL
7½ oz.	can tomato sauce	213 mL
1	pkg. spaghetti sauce mix (I like Lawry's)	1
½ lb.	lasagne noodles	
1 cup	cottage cheese	250 g
½-1 lb.	mozzarella cheese, sliced	250 mL
½ cup	grated Parmesan cheese	250-500 g
		125 mL

Brown meat with seasonings. Add tomatoes, tomato sauce and spaghetti sauce mix. Simmer 20-30 minutes.

Cook noodles until tender, drain into strainer and rinse with cold water.

Layer in 13 x 9" (33 x 22 cm) baking dish: ⅓ sauce, then ½ noodles, then cottage cheese; again ⅓ sauce, ½ noodles then sliced mozzarella. Finally add the last ⅓ sauce. Sprinkle all over top with Parmesan cheese.

Bake until hot and bubbly, about 40 minutes. Serve with hot sliced French bread and a tossed salad with an oil and lemon dressing, page 38.

note: I sometimes slip a layer of thinly sliced zucchini under the mozzarella and it's great!

sweet and sour meatballs Ø

yield: 8-10 servings

Preheat oven 400°F (200°C)

— hamburger with a touch of class!

2 lbs.	lean ground beef	1 kg
1	egg, slightly beaten	1
2 tsp.	salt	10 mL
¼ tsp.	ginger	1 mL
¼ tsp.	black pepper	1 mL
2 tbsp.	milk	30 mL
⅓ cup	dry bread crumbs	75 mL
14 oz.	can pineapple chunks	398 mL
½	medium green pepper, sliced	½
1	large onion, sliced	1
2 tbsp.	butter	30 mL
2 tbsp.	soy sauce	30 mL
2 tbsp.	vinegar	30 mL
2 tbsp.	cornstarch	30 mL
2 tbsp.	water	30 mL

Mix first 7 ingredients and form into balls about 1½" (3.8 cm) in diameter. Place in shallow, greased, 13 x 9" (33 x 22 cm) casserole and bake for about 20 minutes until brown. Turn gently after 10 minutes.

Drain pineapple, RESERVING juice. Add water to juice to make 1 cup (250 mL) liquid. Sauté green pepper and onion with butter in frying pan. Add liquid, pineapple chunks, soy sauce and vinegar. Bring mixture to a boil. Mix cornstarch with water and stir into mixture. Continue stirring until mixture is thickened. Pour over meatballs and bake in 350°F (180°C) oven until hot, about 20-30 minutes.

Serve with rice. This recipe makes about 48 meatballs.

note: — When in a rush, I have just made small hamburger patties for this recipe.
— The meatballs may be browned in a skillet. I just find it easier and less messy in the oven.

61

meat loaf - italian-style ∅

yield: 10-12 servings

Preheat oven 350°F (180°C)

— with lots of pizzazz! Prepare yourself for compliments.

1½ lbs.	lean ground beef	750 g
½ lb.	sausage meat OR ground pork	250 g
2	eggs	2
½ cup	dry bread crumbs	125 mL
1 cup	tomato OR clamato juice	250 mL
½ tsp.	oregano	2 mL
¼ tsp.	black pepper	1 mL
½ tsp.	garlic powder	2 mL
2	small onions, minced	2
8 slices	cooked ham	8 slices
½ lb.	mozzarella cheese, grated	250 g
½ cup	chili sauce	125 mL
½ tsp.	liquid smoke flavoring (optional)	2 mL

Combine first 9 ingredients and mix well. Line a jelly-roll pan, 10 x 15" (25 x 38 cm), with foil. Flatten meat mixture onto foil. Layer ham and cheese on top of meat. Roll your meat loaf jelly-roll fashion, removing foil as you do it. (This procedure is easier than it sounds so don't be discouraged). Pinch final seam closed. Top with chili sauce mixed with smoke flavoring.

Bake for 1 hour.

note: — Use extra beef instead of sausage meat, if desired.
— This recipe may easily be halved. However, leftovers can be frozen in small portions and used for making sand-wiches or a "quick-fix dinner".

It is much easier to be critical than correct.

burgers à la burgundy Ø

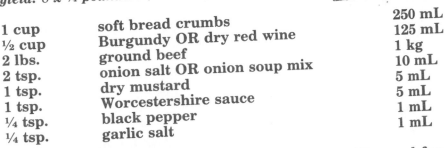

yield: 8 x ¼ pounders (8 x 125 g)

1 cup	soft bread crumbs	250 mL
½ cup	Burgundy OR dry red wine	125 mL
2 lbs.	ground beef	1 kg
2 tsp.	onion salt OR onion soup mix	10 mL
1 tsp.	dry mustard	5 mL
1 tsp.	Worcestershire sauce	5 mL
¼ tsp.	black pepper	1 mL
¼ tsp.	garlic salt	1 mL

Mix all ingredients together well. Shape into patties and fry, broil or barbecue.

chinese hamburger

yield: 8-10 servings

Preheat oven 350°F (180°C)

— *a super recipe - enough for the whole fraternity, but leftovers freeze well.*

1½ lbs.	ground beef	750 g
2	celery stalks, chopped	2
1	small onion, chopped	1
10 oz.	can chicken gumbo soup	284 mL
10 oz.	can cream of mushroom soup	284 mL
10 oz.	can cream of chicken soup	284 mL
6 oz.	pkg. chow mein noodles	170 g

Brown beef with celery and onion in skillet. Drain off excess fat. Put into a 13 x 9" (33 x 22 cm) casserole. Add remaining ingredients, reserving ⅓ noodles for top. Mix well.

Bake, uncovered, 30-40 minutes until hot.

Top with reserved noodles and return to oven for 5 minutes.

hamburger pie

yield 4-6 servings:

— tasty, colorful and easy to prepare!

Preheat oven 350°F (180°C)

1 lb.	lean ground beef	
1	medium onion, chopped	500 g
	salt and pepper, to taste	1
12½ oz.	pkg. frozen green beans	
10 oz.	can tomato soup	350 g
5	potatoes, cooked	284 mL
½ cup	warm milk	5
1	egg, beaten	125 mL
	salt and pepper, to taste	1

Brown beef and onion in skillet and season with salt and pepper. Drain off excess fat.

Cook beans, drain and add to meat mixture. Add tomato soup, mix, and pour mixture into a 4-cup (1 L) greased casserole.

Mash potatoes, add remaining ingredients. Spoon in mounds over meat mixture in casserole. Bake 30-40 minutes.

variation:
A dash of curry adds to the flavor.

minestrone casserole Ø

yield: 6 servings

— when you're really in a hurry!

1½ lbs.	ground beef	
¾ cup	chopped onion	750 g
1	garlic clove, minced	175 mL
2 x 10 oz.	cans minestrone soup	1
14 oz.	can pork and beans	2 x 284 mL
1½ cups	chopped celery	398 mL
1 tbsp.	Worcestershire sauce	375 mL
½ tsp.	crushed oregano	15 mL
		2 mL

In a large frying pan, cook beef, onion and garlic. Drain off fat.

Add remaining ingredients to meat mixture and simmer, covered, until hot - about 15 minutes.

note: Check recipe for minestrone hodgepodge soup, page 23, pictured on page 48A, for a super way to use up leftovers.

taco burgers - olé Ø

yield: 6-8 servings

1½ lbs.	ground beef	750 g
1	pkg. taco seasoning (Lawry's)	1
	sliced French bread	
	shredded lettuce	
	grated Cheddar cheese	
	mild taco sauce	

Combine beef and seasoning mix (you may prefer to use ½ pkg.). Mix well. Form into 6-8 patties. Fry, broil or barbecue.

Serve on French bread, toasted on 1 side. Top with lettuce, cheese and taco sauce.

burger toppings

traditional — tomato, lettuce, cheese, relish, pickle, onion, ketchup, mustard.

groovy — avocado, green pepper, Swiss cheese, bean/alfalfa sprouts, bacon, chili sauce or maybe even guacamole.

To err is human, but when the eraser wears out before the pencil, you could be overdoing it.

macaroni, tomato and beef casserole Ø

yield: 6 servings

— pasta with lots of pep!

Preheat oven 350°F (180°C)

1 lb.	ground beef	
2 cups	raw macaroni	500 g
½ cup	chopped onion	500 mL
1 clove	garlic, minced	125 mL
½ cup	chopped green pepper	1 clove
½ cup	vegetable oil	125 mL
1 tsp.	salt	125 mL
¼ tsp.	black pepper	5 mL
2 tbsp.	Worcestershire sauce	1 mL
2½ cups	tomato juice	30 mL
		625 mL

Brown beef in skillet. Remove to a 6-cup (1.5 L) casserole. Put macaroni, onion, garlic, green pepper and oil in skillet, over medium heat, and stir until the macaroni is yellow, watch carefully. Add to casserole. Heat remaining ingredients in saucepan and pour over all.

Bake 30-40 minutes.

note: — The ½ cup (125 mL) oil is correct, the macaroni soaks up a lot!
— Add beef broth to leftovers for a hearty soup.

variation:

You may also add 1 cup (250 mL) grated Cheddar cheese before baking.

You never get a second chance to make a good first impression.

chuckwagon stew Ø

yield: 4-6 servings

Preheat oven 425°F (220°C)

— *with rootin-tootin beans!*

½ cup	chopped celery	125 mL
¼ cup	chopped onion	50 mL
¼ cup	chopped green pepper	50 mL
1 lb.	lean ground beef	500 g
14 oz.	can pork and beans	398 mL
¼ cup	ketchup	50 mL
¼ cup	water	50 mL
½ tsp.	salt	2 mL
½ tsp.	garlic salt	2 mL

Toss celery, onion and green pepper into a 4-6 cup (1-1.5 L) casserole. Crumble raw beef on top. Bake, uncovered, for 20 minutes.

Remove from oven, stir in remaining ingredients. Return to oven until heated through or about 10-15 minutes.

variation:
May be topped with unbaked Bisquick biscuits and baked another 15 minutes.

smorgasbord meatballs Ø

yield 24-30 meatballs

Preheat oven 350°F (180°C)

¾ lb.	ground beef	365 g
¼ lb.	ground pork OR sausage	125 g
½ cup	soft bread crumbs	125 mL
1	egg, slightly beaten	1
½ cup	unsweetened applesauce	125 mL
2 tbsp.	grated onion	30 mL
1 tsp.	salt	5 mL
⅛ tsp.	cayenne OR dash of Tabasco sauce (optional)	0.5 mL
¼ cup	water	50 mL
¼ cup	ketchup	50 mL

Mix first 8 ingredients together well and form into bite-size balls. Brown in hot fat, turning gently and often. Place in shallow baking dish.

Combine water and ketchup and pour over meatballs. Bake about 30 minutes. Serve hot with toothpicks!

note: Meatballs may also be browned by baking in a 400°F (200°C) oven for 20 minutes.

pork

baked ham

yield: 5-7 lb. (2.5-3.5 kg) with bone — 10-12 servings

Traditionally served with scalloped potatoes and hot mustard.

The bone-in variety is our favorite so that we can make a pot of split-pea soup later. If you are not interested in making soup, look for a "semi-bone-less" butt cut or boneless shank end which has little bone and is very easy to carve. To save on clean-up, I like to line my baking pan with foil!

Bake ham in a shallow pan (with a rack preferably), fat side up.

Bake at 325°F (160°C) for 20-25 minutes/lb. (500g). For a 7-5 lb. (2.5-3.5 kg) ham with bone in, your meat thermometer should register 160°C when done.

"Ready-to-eat" hams or "fully cooked" hams may be eaten as is, but look and taste better if heated at 325°F (160°C) in a shallow pan to 140°C on your meat thermometer, about 15-20 minutes/lb. (500 g).

Optional: Remove rind and score the top of ham (make criss-cross slits in the fat) and insert whole cloves.

During the last hour of baking, baste with mixture of:

1 cup	brown sugar	250 mL
¼ cup	prepared mustard	50 mL
½ cup	beer	125 mL

note: — Cut recipe in half for a small ham.
— WARNING - your kitchen will smell a bit like a brewery!

PLEASE DON'T STRAIGHTEN
THE MESS ON MY DESK
YOU'LL GOOF UP MY SYSTEM

hot mustard

— an old family recipe.

2 tsp.	dry mustard	10 mL
2 tsp.	flour	10 mL
1 tsp.	white sugar	5 mL
	salt and pepper, to taste	
	boiling water	
	vinegar	

Mix together mustard, flour, sugar, salt and pepper, add just enough boiling water to make a thick paste, then thin it by adding vinegar. It's hot! Use sparingly, but do use it.

pork and mushroom casserole Ø

yield: 6-8 servings   *Preheat oven 350°F (180°C)*

— an extra special family favorite - count on serving second helpings.

3 slices	bacon, diced	3 slices
10 oz.	can mushrooms, drained, reserve liquid	284 mL
1	onion, chopped	1
1-2 lb.	pork tenderloin, sliced in 1" (2.5 cm) slices, flattened to ½" (1.3 cm)*	500 g - 1 kg
1	eggs, slightly beaten	2
2	cracker crumbs	250 mL
1 cup	reserved mushroom liquid**	50 mL
¼ cup		

Pan-fry bacon until browned. Set aside, leaving fat in pan. Sauté mushrooms and onions in bacon fat. Remove from pan and combine with bacon.

Dip sliced tenderloin in egg, then crumbs. Brown in skillet in remaining bacon fat (you may have to add more oil).

To put it all together, put a layer of tenderloin in a shallow pan, top with a layer of onion, mushroom and bacon mix and then repeat layers. Add liquid, cover and bake for 40 minutes.

* Pork tenderloin may be purchased whole or "Frenched" which means 1" (2.5 cm) portions that have been flattened with a cleaver or mallet.
** If you use fresh mushrooms, you may use white wine or broth for your liquid.

budget note: Pork cutlets can be used instead of tenderloin.

wieners with onions and peppers Ø

yield: 4-5 servings

— when you are looking for a new way to serve wieners or sausages - this is it!

4 cups	sliced onions	
1	medium green pepper, slivered	1 L
1	garlic clove, minced	1
3 tbsp.	vegetable oil	1
½ tsp.	salt	45 mL
⅛ tsp.	black pepper	2 mL
2 tbsp.	Worcestershire sauce	0.5 mL
1 tbsp.	prepared mustard	30 mL
1 lb.	wieners OR sausage	15 mL
		500 g

Sauté onion, pepper and garlic in oil. Simmer, covered, for about 10 minutes.

Add remaining ingredients to mixture, cutting up wieners (or leave whole). Cover, heat 10 minutes. Serve on or with rice.

saucy sausage casserole Ø

yield: 4-5 servings

Preheat oven 350°F (180°C)

1 lb.	pork sausage (bulk)*	
1 cup	raw rice	500 g
2 x 2 oz.	pkg. chicken noodle soup mix	250 mL
¼ cup	chopped onion	2 x 56 g
1 cup	sliced celery	50 mL
2½ cups	water	250 mL
1 tbsp.	soy sauce	625 mL
½ cup	slivered almonds (optional)	15 mL
		125 mL

Brown sausage meat in skillet. Pour off excess fat.

Place rice, soup mix, onion and celery in 2-quart (2 L) casserole with sausage. Mix water and soy sauce and add to casserole. Mix well. Top with almonds. Cover and bake until rice is tender, 45 minutes to 1 hour.

* You can also use 1 lb. (500 g) of pork sausages - just squish meat out of casing, or use chopped sausages if you are short of time.

variation:

Casserole may be topped with additional, browned whole sausages, before baking, for a heartier meal!

barbecued sausage Ø

yield: 6-8 servings

Preheat oven 350°F (180°C)

— *a spicy sauce adds zip to an oven-baked dish.*

2 lbs.	sausage	1 kg
2 tbsp.	vegetable oil	30 mL
2	onions, finely chopped	2
1½ cups	water	325 mL
1 cup	chili sauce	250 mL
½ cup	brown sugar	125 mL
½ tsp.	dry mustard	2 mL
½ tsp.	salt	2 mL

Brown sausage in skillet and drain off fat. Remove meat from skillet.

Sauté onions in oil until slightly yellow. Add remaining ingredients to skillet and bring to a boil.

Place sausages in a shallow baking dish, top with sauce and bake for 30 minutes.

variation:
Put the sausages back into the skillet with the sauce and simmer until serving time.

barbecued spareribs

yield: 1 lb. (500 g) — 2 servings

Tenderize ribs by simmering in water to cover and 2 tbsp. (30 mL) of vinegar in a covered skillet until tender, ¾-1 hour or by baking at 350°F (180°C) in a covered pan. Drain off excess liquid.

oven method

Brush precooked ribs with a prepared barbecue sauce or go all out and prepare the sauce, see recipe page 21. Return to oven for about ½ hour, basting with more sauce every 10 minutes.

to barbecue

Place precooked ribs on grill, bone side down, over moderate heat. Cook for about 10-15 minutes then brush with prepared barbecue sauce or our delicious homemade variety, see recipe page 21. Finish cooking with the flesh side down. Watch carefully! Total barbecue time: 20-25 minutes.

barbecued pork butt steak

These steaks are relatively inexpensive - be sure to choose those without too much bone or fat.

Marinate for 20-30 minutes (I use the packaged marinades for these). Drain and barbecue about 20 minutes. Sear each side over moderate-high heat and then turn to low until traces of pink have vanished.

See photograph page 80A.

variation:

You can also dip these steaks (without using marinade) in egg wash, then bread crumbs and bake at 375°F (190°C) for about 45 minutes.

barbecue hints:

— Use a spray bottle of water for flare-ups on charcoal barbecues.

— Use baking soda on gas barbecue flare-ups - NEVER WATER.

— Skewered foods should all require same cooking time. I usually do vegetables on one skewer and meat on another.

— Trim excess fat from meats.

— Meats are usually seared on both sides first to seal in the juices, then cooked on lower heat until done (or lower and raise grills to adjust heat).

— Less tender cuts of meat are marinated before barbecuing

— Grills should be oiled before using them.

Work is the greatest thing in the world,
so we should always save some of it for tomorrow.

sweet and sour riblets Ø

yield: 4-5 servings

Preheat oven 350°F (180°C)

1½ cups	brown sugar	375 mL
½ cup	vinegar	125 mL
1 cup	water	250 mL
1 tsp.	soy sauce	5 mL
2 tbsp.	cornstarch	30 mL
2 tbsp.	water	30 mL
1 tbsp.	soy sauce	15 mL
2 lbs.	pork riblets	1 kg
	flour	
	salt and pepper, to taste	
2-3 tbsp.	vegetable oil	30-45 mL

Bring first 4 ingredients to a boil in saucepan. Mix next 3 ingredients together and add to hot sauce. Boil 4-5 minutes. Watch carefully. Remove from heat.

Roll riblets in flour seasoned with salt and pepper. Brown in 2-3 tbsp. (30-45 mL) of hot oil in a skillet. Place the browned ribs in a shallow baking dish. Pour sauce over and bake for 1 hour, basting occasionally.

See photograph page 32A.

pork chops (or chicken) with rice Ø

yield: 4-6 servings

Preheat oven 375°F (190°C)

— a real winner! Serve with a tossed salad for a very tasty dinner.

1 cup	uncooked rice	250 mL
10 oz.	can cream of mushroom soup OR	284 mL
	cream of chicken soup	
1½ oz.	pkg. dry onion soup mix	40 g
1¾ cups	milk OR boiling water	425 mL
4-6	pork chops OR	4-6
1	frying chicken, cut-up	1
	paprika	

Mix rice, soups and liquid together then pour into a 13 x 9" (33 x 22 cm) casserole.

Place pork chops (or if using chicken, rinse off and pat dry then place skin side down) on top of rice. Cover and bake for 45 minutes. Uncover. (If using chicken, turn skin side up and sprinkle with paprika.) Return to oven for an additional 15 minutes. Broil 2-3 minutes if desired, to brown the meat.

poultry

thanksgiving dinner for 2

As I recall, exams always conflicted with the Thanksgiving holiday. Would you believe we even put holes in the bottom of a can to strain the gravy - you only do that once - that leaves 2 choices, buy a strainer or learn to make good gravy!

menu

Cornish game hens
wild rice casserole, page 32
mandarin salad
banana split pie/fudge sauce, page 101

To prepare hens: allow 1 hen / serving

Wash inside and out thoroughly. Pat dry. Season with lemon juice, seasoning salt and pepper. Put in roasting pan and bake at 400°F (200°C) for 1 hour. (Almost forgot - brush all with melted butter). Baste occasionally with drippings.

note: They may also be split in half and baked (flesh side up).

To prepare salad:

Mix shredded lettuce with spanish onion rings (red onions are also great) and drained mandarin oranges. Top with Italian dressing to taste.

To complete the feast, how about hot rolls, maybe even some poultry dressing (made from the packaged mixes) and don't forget the cranberry jelly!

Tact is the ability to see others as they see themselves.

74

how to cut up a chicken

objective: to cut up 1 chicken.

apparatus: — one innocent, slippery, uncooked chicken.
          — a sharp knife.

attitude: grin and bear it!

procedure: — Wash chicken and pat dry.
          — Anchor the beast on your cutting board.
          — Remove giblets, save for soup or dressing, feed to cat, or discard.
          — Cut off each leg where they latch onto the thigh bone.
          — Cut off thighs at end of thigh bone.
          — Snip off the tips of the wings and discard.
          — Slash wings from body at joints.
          — Latch on to the part that goes over the fence last and carefully divide the back from the breast between back bones and breast bones.
          — Split back into two sections.
          — Slice the breast in two along the breast bone, then cut these in two if desired.

(Hurrah! I knew you could do it!)

oven-baked chicken

yield: 5-6 servings

preheat oven 400°F (200°C)

—finger-lickin good!

½ cup	butter or margarine	125 mL
	frying chicken, cut-up	
	seasoning salt, to taste	
dash	garlic salt (optional)	dash

Melt the butter in a 13 x 9" (33 x 22 cm) baking dish. (Just set your pan in the oven for a few minutes to do this.)

Wash chicken pieces and pat dry. Dip pieces in melted butter and then place skin side up in baking dish. Season with seasoning salt and garlic (if desired).

Bake, uncovered, for 1 hour.

Serve with a smile (and serviettes). Super for a picnic in the park (or your backyard)!

chicken and mushroom casserole

yield: 5-6 servings

preheat oven 400°F (200°C)

— one of my Mom's favorites. Soda cracker crumbs provide a special flavor.

1	chicken, cut-up	
	soda crackers, crushed	1
10 oz.	can mushroom soup	
½ cup	milk	284 mL
		125 mL

Simply wash chicken and pat dry. Dip chicken pieces in egg wash (see below) then into cracker crumbs. Put chicken pieces in a shallow greased baking dish. Bake until brown, about 45 minutes.

Mix soup with milk and pour over chicken. Cover lightly with foil and bake another 15 minutes.

egg wash

¼ cup	milk	50 mL
2	eggs, slightly beaten	2
1 tsp.	seasoning salt	5 mL

Stir all ingredients together.

The trouble with good advice is that it usually interferes with our plans.

chicken divan Ø

preheat oven 350°F (180°C)

yield: 4 servings

— an old favorite - chicken dressed up in a delightful sauce.

2	broccoli stalks OR 1 small pkg. frozen broccoli	2
2	whole chicken breasts, cooked, boned, halved*	2
10 oz.	can cream of chicken soup	284 mL
½	beef cube, dissolved in 2 tbsp. (30 mL) water	½
½ cup	mayonnaise	125 mL
1½ tsp.	lemon juice	7 mL
¼ tsp.	curry powder	1 mL
¼ cup	grated old Cheddar cheese	50 mL
	buttered bread crumbs	

Cook broccoli just until tender. Put in a 4-6 cup (1-1.5 L) buttered casserole and layer cooked chicken on top.

Mix remaining ingredients, except cheese and crumbs. Pour over chicken. Top with grated cheese and crumbs.

Bake for about 30 minutes until hot.

* to cook chicken - brown quickly in butter in skillet, add a bit of diced onion and water (or chicken broth) and simmer until cooked, about 15 minutes. The meat may be removed from the bone before or after cooking.

variation:
If broccoli is not your favorite, you could try using peas and carrots or beans, etc.!

Some men see things as they are and say, why?
I dream things that never were and say, why not?

Robert F. Kennedy

skillet chicken niçoise

yield: 4-6 servings

— an elegant skillet dinner.

3 lbs.	chicken, cut up	1.5 kg
¼ cup	olive oil OR vegetable oil	50 mL
2	onions, quartered	2
¼ tsp.	thyme*	1 mL
2	garlic cloves , minced	2
3-4	tomatoes, chopped OR 28 oz. (796 mL) can tomatoes, drained	3-4
⅔ cup	dry white wine OR chicken broth	150 mL
6	parsley stems OR 1 tbsp. (15 mL) dried parsley	6
	broccoli florets, cooked	
	black olives, drained	

Wash the chicken and pat dry. Season with salt and pepper.

In large skillet, heat 2 tbsp. (30 mL) oil, add onions and thyme, brown lightly. Transfer to a bowl. Add 2 tbsp. (30 mL) oil to skillet and brown chicken pieces. Remove chicken pieces and set aside.

Sauté garlic in skillet for 30 seconds. Do not brown. Add tomatoes, wine and parsley to skillet along with onions and chicken - skin side up.

Bring liquid to a boil, then simmer, covered, for 30 minutes. Remove chicken breasts, simmer for another 30 minutes.

To thicken the sauce, remove cover and cook over moderate heat for 10 minutes to reduce amount of liquid. Replace chicken breasts in skillet, cover and reheat.

Garnish with tender-crisp broccoli and black olives just before serving.

* If you do not have "thyme" seasoning, don't panic - take "time" to make it anyway - but do try it with "thyme" sometime!

See photograph on front cover.

chicken wings

yield: — 2.2 lbs. (1 kg) — approximately 14 wings — 28 pieces
— depending on whether you are making a meal or appetizers and whether you are a football player or a cheerleader, it's difficult to say the number of servings per lb. or kilogram. I will let you be the judge!

— fun to make, a delight to eat and inexpensive - however, if they are not meaty enough for you, just use the same recipes for thighs or drumsticks!

chicken wings #1 Ø

yield: approx. 12 wings

preheat oven 400°F (200°C)

2.2 lbs.	chicken wings	1 kg
⅓ cup	soy sauce	75 mL
1½ oz.	pkg. Shake'n Bake for chicken	42 g
	warmed honey for glaze	

Wash chicken and pat dry. Cut wings at joints and discard tips if desired or leave whole. Now, all you do is marinate the wings in the soy sauce for 1-2 hours, turning once or twice. Drain.

Put Shake'n Bake in a plastic bag, toss in wings and shake well. Remove wings and put in a shallow greased baking dish. Bake for 30 minutes.

Before serving, brush with honey.

note: Also great done on the barbecue.

See photograph page 80A.

A teddy bear can be your best friend - he accepts you as you are and never outgrows you intellectually.

chicken wings #2 Ø

yield: approx. 12 wings
(24 pieces trimmed)

preheat oven 425°F (220°C)

2.2 lbs.	chicken wings	
2	eggs, well beaten	1 kg
2 tbsp.	water	2
¾ cup	flour	30 mL
¼ cup	butter, melted	175 mL
½ cup	oil	50 mL
2 tbsp.	soy sauce	125 mL
2 tbsp.	water	30 mL
⅔ cup	white sugar	30 mL
⅓ cup	vinegar	150 mL
1 tsp.	seasoning salt	75 mL

Remove wing tips. Cut wings at joint. Beat eggs with water. Put butter and oil in shallow roasting pan. Dip wings in egg mixture, then in flour. Put in pan, turning once to coat with oil. Brown in oven (20-25 minutes). Wings could also be browned in frying pan and then baked with sauce.

Mix remaining ingredients in a small pot, over low heat. When the wings are browned, drain off excess fat and pour sauce over them. Return to oven for 10-15 minutes, basting with sauce 2 or 3 times.

chicken noodle casserole Ø

yield: 6 servings

preheat oven 350°F (180°C)

— add this recipe to your "easy to prepare" category.

2	cooked chicken breasts*	2
1 cup	cooked noodles	250 mL
1 cup	diced celery	250 mL
10 oz.	can cream of mushroom OR chicken soup	284 mL
½ cup	mayonnaise	
3 tbsp.	milk	125 mL
½ cup	slivered almonds (optional)	45 mL
2 oz.	pkg. barbecued chips	125 mL
		55 g

Remove bone from chicken breasts and cut meat in bite-size pieces. Combine all ingredients, except chips, and pour into a 13 x 9" (33 x 22 cm) casserole. Top with crushed chips (puncture bag and roll with a rolling pin or jar).

Bake for 30-45 minutes just until hot.

* Or other leftover cooked chicken or turkey.

a barbecue to feed the whole team

make your own casserole Ø

yield: 6 servings

Preheat oven 350°F (180°C)

— here is a great chance to use your imagination - green peppers, mushrooms, broccoli, peas, etc. may be added. Just use your favorites. Also a super way to use up leftovers!

6 oz.	pkg. macaroni OR noodles	175 g
2 cups	cubed ham, chicken OR tuna, etc.	500 mL
10 oz.	can cream soup of your choice	284 mL
1 cup	milk	250 mL
½ cup	chopped onion	125 mL
½ cup	cubed old Cheddar cheese	125 mL
½ tsp.	salt	2 mL
2 oz.	pkg. potato chips, crushed (barbecue are great)	55 g

Cook macaroni, drain and rinse with cold water. Put into a greased 6-8 cup (1.5-2 L) casserole. Add all other ingredients, except chips.

Sprinkle crushed chips on top. Bake until hot, 30-40 minutes.

a little at a time

We sometimes grow discouraged
When the things we want to do
Seem to take a whole lot longer
Than we'd really like them to. . .
If there's a goal that must be reached,
Or a bridge that must be crossed
We feel that in the time it takes
Our purpose will be lost.
But if something is worth doing,
Then the only way to do it
Is just a little at a time -
And when you're finally through it,
You'll find it was less difficult
To do (without a doubt)
Than you ever had imagined
Before you started out.
So if there's a dream that should come true
Or a mountain you would climb,
Remember that great things are done
A little at a time.

macaroni and cheese Ø

yield: 6 servings

— a sophisticated version!

Preheat oven 350°F (180°C)

2 tbsp.	butter	
¼ cup	chopped onion	30 mL
¼ cup	chopped celery	50 mL
10 oz.	can mushroom soup	50 mL
⅓ cup	milk	284 mL
2½-3 cups	grated old Cheddar cheese	75 mL
3 cups	cooked macaroni, drained, use 1½ cups (375 mL) raw macaroni	625-750 mL
		750 mL
1 tsp.	dry mustard	
dash	Worcestershire sauce	5 mL
	salt and pepper, to taste	dash

Sauté onion and celery in butter just until onion is transparent. Combine all ingredients, reserving ½ cup (125 mL) cheese for top, mix well and place in 6-cup (1.5 L) greased casserole.

Bake until heated through, stirring once. Top with reserved cheese. Return to oven and bake for an additional 10-15 minutes or until cheese is lightly browned and bubbly.

variation:
Chopped fresh tomato, leftover ham, sausage, etc. could be added.

did you know? — That a wee bit of oil added to the water for cooking pasta will help prevent it from boiling over.
— Pasta is always rinsed with cold water after being cooked and drained.

I like work - it fascinates me, I can sit and look at it for hours.

pizza

yield: 4-6 servings

Preheat oven 425°F (220°C)

— crisp crust for 1 thick or 2 thin 12" (30 cm) crusts.

crust

2⅔ cups	flour	650 mL
⅓ cup	grated Parmesan cheese	75 mL
2½ tsp.	baking powder	12 mL
1 tsp.	salt	5 mL
¼ cup	cold margarine	50 mL
¼ cup	lard	50 mL
¾ cup	milk	175 mL

Combine dry ingredients. Cut in margarine and lard with a pastry blender until mixture resembles coarse crumbs. Gradually blend in milk until a ball of dough starts to form (using a fork for blending). Form dough into a ball.

On a floured surface, roll dough out into a circle to fit your pizza pan. Fit dough into pan and partially bake for 8-10 minutes. Remove from oven and cool.

topping

1 cup	tomato sauce	250 mL
2 cups	shredded mozzarella cheese	500 mL
	sliced meat of your choice	
	green pepper, sliced	
	mushrooms, sliced	
	anchovies, etc.	
	oregano OR Italian herb mix	
	(optional)	

Top pizza shell with a thin layer of tomato sauce. Layer with 1 cup (250 mL) cheese, meat, green pepper, mushrooms, anchovies, etc. (the choice is yours!). Top with remaining cup of cheese.

Bake for 20 minutes.

fish

a few "fishy" ideas

— *These ideas have been included because they say fish is good food for thinking! Fish should be eaten when ready - it is not a "keep-hot-in-the-oven" dish. Allow ⅓-½ lb. (175-250 g) per serving with the bone in or ¼ lb. (125 g) boned.*

Always wash well and wipe dry.

pan-fried fish

yield: 4-5 servings

— *serve with wedges of lemon or tartar sauce.*

1 lb.	fish fillets	500 g
	flour	
1	egg	1
¼ cup	milk	50 mL
¼ tsp.	salt	1 mL
	bread OR cracker crumbs	
3-4 tbsp.	salad oil	45-60 mL

Coat fillets with flour. Beat egg, milk and salt together. Dip fillets in egg mixture then in crumbs.

Heat oil in skillet and brown fish on both sides, about 2-3 minutes per side, depending on the thickness. If cooking thicker fish steaks, turn heat down after browning and cook until the juice is opaque and the flesh flakes easily.

note: I sometimes toss a bit of lemon juice into the pan just before serving.

variation:
You can add a bit of Parmesan cheese to your crumbs.

oven-baked fish Ø

yield: 1 lb. (500 g) boneless - 4 servings   *preheat oven 425°F (220°C)*

Place fish in a shallow greased casserole. Season with salt and pour melted butter on top. Sprinkle with paprika (optional) and add a bit of water. Bake in oven until the juice is opaque and the flesh flakes easily. (See note below).

variations:
1. When fish is tender add more butter and broil, just until crisp on top.
2. To pep up your butter, for each ½ cup (125 mL) butter you could add 1 of the following: 1 tsp. (5 mL) of anchovy paste, 2 tbsp. (30 mL) chopped green onion, 2 tsp. (10 mL) prepared mustard, or 1 tbsp. (15 mL) lemon juice.
3. Bake with a creole sauce made by adding bits of sautéed celery, onion and green pepper to canned tomatoes or tomato sauce - using a dash of lemon juice or Tabasco sauce, if desired.

barbecued fish

Brush fillets lightly with soy sauce and marinate with an oil and vinegar dressing for 30 minutes, then barbecue - don't forget to grease the grill - please!

note: A general rule of thumb is that fish is cooked for 10 minutes for each 1" (2.5 cm) of thickness at medium-high heat - 425°F (220°C).

To entertain some people all you have to do is listen.

tuna casserole ∅

yield: 4 servings

— if all the previous ideas are too "fishy" try this recipe.

2 cups	cooked noodles	500 mL
7.5 oz.	can tuna, crab OR salmon	225 g
10 oz.	can mushroom soup	284 mL
5 oz.	milk	150 mL
2 oz.	pkg. potato chips, crushed	55 g

Combine noodles and tuna. Dilute mushroom soup with milk and combine with tuna mixture. Pour into a 6-cup (1.5 L) greased casserole and top with crushed potato chips.

Bake at 350°F (180°C) for 20-30 minutes until hot.

variation:
Use crushed barbecue chips.

salmon casserole ∅

yield: 6-8 servings

preheat oven 375°F (190°C)

— a tried and true recipe - easy to put together and so easy to eat - a real winner. You can also use tuna or crabmeat.

8 oz.	noodles	250 g
¼ cup	mayonnaise	50 mL
2 x 7.5 oz.	cans salmon	2 x 225 g
¼ cup	chopped onion (optional)	50 mL
10 oz.	pkg. frenched green beans	283 g
10 oz.	can mushroom OR celery soup	284 mL
½ cup	milk	125 mL
2-3 cups	shredded OR sliced mozzarella cheese	500-750 mL

Cook noodles according to package directions. Drain noodles and mix in mayonnaise. Pour into a greased 13 x 9" (33 x 22 cm) casserole.

Drain salmon, mash with a fork, add chopped onion (if desired) and layer on top of noodles.

Cook beans, drain and spread over salmon. Dilute soup with milk and spread over all.

Bake 30 minutes until hot. Remove from oven, top with mozzarella. Return to oven, bake until bubbly and brown. Watch carefully!

Toss a green salad together, relax and enjoy a scrumptious meal.

oatmeal cake with broiled icing

yield: 8-10 servings

Preheat oven 350°F (180°C)

—moist, delicious and nutritious!

1¼ cups	boiling water	300 mL
1 cup	rolled oats, quick cooking	250 mL
½ cup	margarine	125 mL
1 cup	brown sugar	250 mL
1 cup	white sugar	250 mL
1 tsp.	vanilla	5 mL
2	eggs	2
1⅓ cups	flour	325 mL
1 tsp.	baking soda	5 mL
1 tsp.	nutmeg	5 mL
½ tsp.	salt	2 mL

Pour water over oats and let stand. Cream margarine with the sugars, add vanilla. Beat and blend well. Add eggs, 1 at a time. Beat until light and fluffy.

Combine the remaining dry ingredients and add to sugar/egg mixture then mix well. Add rolled oats to batter. Pour batter into 13 x 9" (33 x 22 cm) pan. Bake for 40 minutes.

broiled icing

— not necessary but scrumptious!

⅓ cup	butter	75 mL
½ cup	sugar	125 mL
¼ cup	brown sugar	50 mL
¼ tsp.	vanilla	1 mL
¼ cup	light cream OR milk	50 mL
1 cup	flaked coconut	250 mL
1 cup	chopped nuts (optional)	250 mL

Melt butter, stir in remaining ingredients and blend well.

Remove cake from oven and turn on broiler. Spread icing on cake and broil until bubbly and brown - watch ever so carefully!

brownie - bonanza

yield: 8 x 8" (20 x 20 cm) pan

Preheat oven 350°F (180°C)

— these delicious brownies have 5 suggested toppings - the choices are yours - have fun!

2 oz.	unsweetened chocolate*	55 g
½ cup	margarine	125 mL
1 cup	sugar	250 mL
2	eggs	2
1 tsp.	vanilla	5 mL
½ cup	flour	125 mL
½ cup	chopped nuts (optional)	125 mL

Melt chocolate and margarine in a saucepan over low heat. Remove from heat. Add sugar. Stir in eggs and vanilla and beat vigorously. Stir in flour and pour all into a greased 8 x 8" (20 x 20 cm) pan.

Bake 20-25 minutes. Do not overbake! Cool before icing with chocolate icing, see recipe below.

* Or use 6 tbsp. (90 mL) cocoa plus an extra 1 tbsp. (15 mL) margarine.

note: These brownies are like fudge. If you wish a cake type - increase flour to ⅔ cup (150 mL) and add ½ tsp. (2 mL) baking powder.

chocolate icing

2 oz.	unsweetened chocolate	55 g
2 tbsp.	butter	30 mL
1 cups	icing sugar	300 mL
2-3 tbsp.	milk, added gradually	30-45 mL
1 tsp.	vanilla	5 mL

Melt chocolate and butter over low heat, remove from heat and add remaining ingredients. Beat well.

variations:

1. Dust top with icing sugar after baking.
2. Sprinkle nuts on top of batter before baking.
3. Top with small marshmallows after baking. Broil until brown, then drizzle with melted chocolate chipits.
4. Top with mint frosting (white frosting with peppermint flavoring and green food coloring added). Cool cake before frosting. Top with a layer of melted chocolate chipits.

See photograph page 96A.

chocolate-cherry layer bars

yield: 13 x 9" (33 x 22 cm) pan

Preheat oven 325°F (160°C)

— always a hit!

½ cup	margarine	125 mL
1½ cups	graham wafer crumbs	375 mL
14 oz.	can Eagle Brand condensed milk	395 mL
1 cup	chocolate chipits	250 mL
1 cup	flaked coconut	250 mL
¾ cup	chopped nuts (optional)	175 mL
¾ cup	glacéd cherries	175 mL

Melt margarine in a 13 x 9" (33 x 22 cm) pan. Add crumbs and mix well. Pat firmly into pan. Pour condensed milk over crumbs. Sprinkle on chipits, coconut, nuts and cherries and pat down firmly with a spatula or fork. Bake 25-30 minutes until lightly browned.

See photograph page 96A.

peanut butter slice

yield: 13 x 9" (33 x 22 cm) pan

Preheat oven 350°F (180°C)

— nutritious and yummy!

¾ cup	margarine	175 mL
⅓ cup	peanut butter	75 mL
1 cup	brown sugar	250 mL
1	egg	1
1 tsp.	vanilla	5 mL
2 cups	flour	500 mL

Mix all ingredients together and pat firmly into a 13 x 9" (33 x 22 cm) pan. Bake for 15-20 minutes. Cool before icing, see recipe below.

chocolate-peanut butter icing

⅔ cup	chocolate chipits	150 mL
½ cup	peanut butter	125 mL

Melt chipits and blend in peanut butter. Spread on top of cooled cake.

butterscotch squares

yield: 8 x 8" (20 x 20 cm) pan

— easy to make (no baking) - easier to eat!

¼ cup	butter	
½ cup	butterscotch chipits*	50 mL
1 tsp.	vanilla	125 mL
1	egg, beaten	5 mL
¼ tsp.	salt	1
¾ cup	coconut	1 mL
½ cup	chopped nuts (optional)	175 mL
2 cups	crushed Dad's cookies OR graham wafer crumbs	125 mL
		500 mL

Melt butter and chipits over low heat. Add remaining ingredients. Mix well and pat into an 8 x 8" (20 x 20 cm) pan. Top with icing, see recipe below.

* You could use chocolate chipits and change the name.

butter icing

2 tbsp.	soft butter	
1 cup	icing sugar	30 mL
1 tbsp.	custard powder (optional, but so good!)	250 mL
		15 mL
½ tsp.	vanilla	
1½ tbsp.	milk	2 mL
		22 mL

Blend all ingredients until smooth. Spread over cake.

note: A knife dipped in hot water helps to spread the icing.

If at first you succeed, try to hide your astonishment.

chewy squares

yield: 13 x 9" (33 x 22 cm) pan

— a crunchy, crispy treat.

2 x 2 oz.	pkg. McIntosh Toffee	2 x 55 g
1½ cups	marshmallows	375 mL
½ cup	margarine	125 mL
1 tbsp.	honey (optional)	15 mL
3½ cups	Rice Krispies	875 mL
3½ cups	slightly crushed Corn Flakes	875 mL

Combine toffee, marshmallows, margarine and honey in a saucepan and cook over medium heat until melted. Remove from heat.

Stir in cereals and pour into a 13 x 9" (33 x 22 cm) pan. Cool.

mud hen bars

yield: 13 x 9" (33 x 22 cm) pan   Preheat oven 350°F (180°C)

— dieters beware!

½ cup	butter OR margarine	125 mL
1 cup	sugar	250 mL
3	eggs, 1 whole, 2 separated	3
1½ cups	flour	375 mL
1 tsp.	baking powder	5 mL
¼ tsp.	salt	1 mL
1 cup	chopped nuts	250 mL
½ cup	chocolate chipits	125 mL
1 cup	miniature marshmallows	250 mL
1 cup	brown sugar	250 mL

Cream together butter and sugar. Beat in whole egg plus 2 egg yolks.

Mix flour, baking powder and salt. Add to creamed mixture. Blend well. Spread in a 13 x 9" (33 x 22 cm) pan.

Sprinkle nuts, chipits and marshmallows over batter.

After all that, you should still have 2 egg whites left (I hope). Beat the egg whites until stiff. Gently fold in brown sugar and spread over batter (a knife dipped in hot water may hasten this process).

Bake 25-30 minutes until golden brown.

See photograph page 96A.

91

butter tarts

yield: 12 tarts

Preheat oven 400°F (200°C)

— almost as good as Mom's!

Time, space and courage do not allow me to teach you to make pastry, but if you treat yourself to frozen tart shells (they are already in their own foil so just put them on a baking sheet) and fill with:

1	large egg	1
1 tsp.	vanilla	5 mL
¼ cup	melted butter, cooled	50 mL
1 cup	brown sugar	250 mL
1 tbsp.	vinegar OR lemon juice	15 mL
¾ cup	currants OR raisins*	175 mL
½ cup	chopped nuts	125 mL

In a bowl, beat egg and combine with remaining ingredients. Fill tart shells ⅔ full and bake 12-15 minutes (watch closely). Let cool and enjoy!

* These are best if soaked in warm water and then drained.

See photograph page 96A.

chocolate chipit bars

yield: 8 x 8" (20 x 20 cm) pan

— NO baking required and better than a chocolate bar!

¾ cup	honey	175 mL
1 cup	peanut butter	250 mL
3 cups	Rice Krispies	750 mL
1 cup	chocolate chipits	250 mL
1 cup	chopped peanuts	250 mL
1 tsp.	vanilla	5 mL

Combine honey and peanut butter and cook over medium heat until it is smooth and just comes to a boil. Remove from heat and stir in remaining ingredients. Pat into an 8 x 8" (20 x 20 cm) pan and chill about 1 hour (if you can wait that long!).

See photograph page 96A.

graham wafer cake

yield: 8 x 8" (20 x 20 cm) pan

— another "no-bake" square, perfect for anyone - anytime!

½ cup	butter OR margarine	125 mL
2 tbsp.	cocoa	30 mL
½ cup	brown sugar	125 mL
1	egg, well beaten	1
2 cups	graham wafer crumbs	500 mL
½ cup	chopped nuts (optional)	125 mL
1 tsp.	vanilla	5 mL

Put butter, cocoa, sugar and egg in a saucepan and cook for 1-2 minutes over medium heat. Stir constantly until smooth. Add remaining ingredients and pack firmly into a greased 8 x 8" (20 x 20 cm) pan. Cool and top with vanilla or chocolate icing (see recipe for Brownies, page 88).

note: — This recipe may be doubled (use same size pan if you want a thicker square which is very good).
— I also prefer to coarsely crush graham wafers for this rather than using prepared crumbs.

peanut butter balls

yield: 30 balls

— when serving, I put these out at the last minute for two reasons — the chocolate may soften and they disappear like magic!

1 cup	peanut butter, crunchy style	250 mL
1 cup	icing sugar	250 mL
2-4 tbsp.	melted butter	30-60 mL
1 cup	Rice Krispies	250 mL
4-6 sq.	semisweet chocolate	112-168 g
1 tbsp.	paraffin wax*	15 mL

Mix peanut butter, icing sugar and butter [the amount of butter will depend on the consistency of your peanut butter - if oily, use only 2 tbsp (30 mL)]. Add Rice Krispies and form into 1" (2.5 cm) balls. Chill. Melt chocolate and shaved wax in top of double boiler (water should be hot, not boiling). Dip balls (I use 2 teaspoons), let excess chocolate drip off and place on cookie sheet lined with wax paper. Cool and store in refrigerator.

*Optional: It just prevents chocolate from softening at room temperature.

crispy oatmeal cookies

yield: 4 dozen - 2½" (6 cm) cookies

— WARNING - these disappear fast!

Preheat oven 350°F (180°C)

1 cup	lard OR margarine	
¾ cup	brown sugar	250 mL
¾ cup	white sugar	175 mL
2	eggs, beaten	175 mL
1 tsp.	vanilla	2
1 tsp.	baking soda	5 mL
1 tbsp.	hot water	5 mL
1½ cups	flour	15 mL
1 tsp.	salt	375 mL
2 cups	rolled oats	5 mL
1 cup	chocolate chipits	500 mL
1 cup	chopped nuts (optional)	250 mL
		250 mL

Cream lard and sugars until fluffy. Add eggs and vanilla.

Dissolve baking soda in water and add to batter.Blend in flour, salt and rolled oats. Stir in chipits and nuts.Drop by teaspoonfuls onto greased cookie sheet and bake 8-10 minutes.

note: Margarine could be used but lard is best in this recipe.

See photograph page 96A.

You have only failed when you have failed to try.

spice cookies

yield: 3 dozen - 2½" (6 cm) cookies

Preheat oven 325°F (160°C)

— exceptionally delicious!

		250 mL
1 cup	sugar	250 mL
1 cup	butter	1
1	egg, beaten	60 mL
4 tbsp.	molasses	500 mL
2 cups	flour	10 mL
2 tsp.	baking soda	2 mL
½ tsp.	salt	5 mL
1 tsp.	cinnamon	5 mL
1 tsp.	ginger	2 mL
½ tsp.	cloves	
	granulated sugar, for dipping	

Cream sugar and butter. Blend egg and molasses with the creamed mixture.

Combine dry ingredients and add to creamed mixture. Mix well.

Put dough in refrigerator until firm (or freezer if you are in a hurry) - this makes the dough less sticky and easier to form into balls.

Pinch off small amounts of dough, form into balls, roll in sugar and place on an ungreased cookie sheet, about 2" (5 cm) apart.

Bake 8-10 minutes. Don't overbake - they should be a bit moist and chewy.

See photograph page 96A.

An alarm clock is a device used to scare the daylights into you.

almond crunch

yield: 24 servings

— never fails!

Preheat oven 325°F (160°C)

½ cup	butter	
1 cup	brown sugar	125 mL
1 tsp.	vanilla	250 mL
1 cup	rolled oats	5 mL
1 tsp.	baking powder	250 mL
1 cup	shredded coconut	5 mL
½ cup	slivered almonds	250 mL
		125 mL

Melt butter and brown sugar in a saucepan. Add remaining ingredients and mix well. Pour into a greased 8 x 8" (20 x 20 cm) pan. Bake 20-25 minutes or until golden brown.

note: Cut while warm.

See photograph page 96A.

frozen chocolate peanut square

yield: 13 x 9" (33 x 22 cm) pan

— do you ever get the craving for one of those chocolate-coated ice cream bars studded with nuts? Fix it ahead and forget about it until you want a treat!

¾ cup	butter	
2 cups	unsifted icing sugar	175 mL
1½ cups	salted peanuts, chopped	500 mL
6 oz.	chocolate chipits, melted	375 mL
2 cups	Dads cookie crumbs	170 g
3	eggs	500 mL
½ gallon	vanilla ice cream, slightly softened	3
		2 L

Melt ¼ cup (50 mL) butter and mix with crumbs. Pat into 13 x 9" (33 x 22 cm) pan. Beat remaining butter with icing sugar until creamy. Beat in eggs, 1 at a time. Add chocolate and blend. Fold in 1 cup (250 mL) peanuts and spread mixture over crust. Freeze until firm. Spread ice cream over top. Sprinkle with ½ cup (125 mL) peanuts. Cover and freeze until firm.

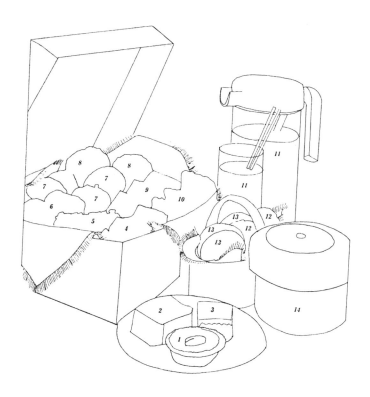

a care package from mom

apple-oatmeal crisp

Preheat oven 350°F (180°C)

— *just had to include this basic recipe. Not only is it delectable, but it can be so versatile (see below).*

2 tbsp.	flour	30 mL
½ cup	sugar	125 mL
5	large apples, sliced (Granny Smith are best)	5

topping:

½ cup	brown sugar	125 mL
½ cup	oatmeal	125 mL
½ cup	flour	125 mL
dash	salt	dash
1 tsp.	cinnamon	5 mL
¼ cup	butter	50 mL

Combine flour, sugar and apples and place in a buttered 6-cup (1.5 L) casserole.

Mix together all dry ingredients for topping and cut in the butter (using a pastry blender or a couple of knives or add chunks of butter and mix gently with your hands).

Spread topping over apples and bake 45 minutes.

Serve warm with ice cream or whipped cream or Cheddar cheese.

variations:
1. Use other fresh fruits such as peaches, blueberries, raspberries, etc.
2. Substitute a can of your favorite pie filling for the apple, sugar and flour base - just don't forget to change the recipe name too!

raspberry ribbon dessert

yield: 12 servings

— mighty tasty and refreshing.

3 oz.	pkg. raspberrry Jell-O	
¼ cup	sugar	85 g
1¼ cups	boiling water	50 mL
10 oz.	pkg. frozen raspberries	300 mL
1 tbsp.	lemon juice	284 g
3 oz.	pkg. cream cheese, softened	15 mL
⅓ cup	icing sugar	85 g
1 tsp.	vanilla	75 mL
dash	salt	5 mL
1 cup	whipping cream, whipped	dash
		250 mL

Dissolve Jell-O and sugar in boiling water. Add raspberries and lemon juice and chill until partially set.

Blend cheese with icing sugar. Add vanilla, salt and whipped cream.

Swirl cheese mixture into Jell-O mixture. Pour into an 8 x 8" (20 x 20 cm) square pan or into a pie plate with a baked graham wafer crust, see recipe page 99.

Money talks, but sometimes a dollar doesn't have enough cents to say much.

crumb crusts

yield: 9" (23 cm) single crust

Preheat oven 375°F (190°C)

— just bake and fill with your favorite fillings.

#1:

1⅓ cups	graham wafer crumbs, plain OR chocolate	325 mL
⅓ cup	butter, melted	75 mL
¼ cup	sugar	50 mL

Mix together; pat firmly into pie plate. Bake at 375°F (190°C) for 8 minutes.

#2:

1¼ cups	crushed Christie chocolate wafers	300 mL
⅓ cup	butter, melted	75 mL

Same method as in #1.

#3:

1	small pkg. crushed Dad's cookies, about 25	1
⅓ cup	butter, melted	75 mL

Same method as in #1.

Geniuses are rarely tidy.

watermelon balls with ginger

yield: 4 servings

— a refreshing simple dessert for all ginger lovers!

¼	watermelon [should yield 2-3 cups (500-750 mL) of balls]	¼
½ cup	water	
¼ cup	green ginger wine*	125 mL
1 tbsp.	sugar	50 mL
1-2 tsp.	slivered preserved ginger	15 mL
	red food coloring (optional)**	5-10 mL

Prepare watermelon balls using melon baller. Combine next 4 ingredients in a pan, stir over medium heat until sugar is dissolved. Cool. Pour over watermelon and refrigerate for several hours or overnight.

* Green ginger wine is available at specialty liquor stores. If you can't find it, use white wine and some of the syrup from the preserved ginger.

** At some seasons of the year, watermelon is very pale, a few drops of red food coloring will give you a colorful dessert.

variation:

You could use the same syrup for pears.

See photograph page 32A.

Even a mosquito doesn't get a slap on the back until he starts working.

banana split pie

yield: 8-10 servings

— how to impress the boyfriend or girlfriend AND yourself!

1	crumb crust, recipe page 99	1
3	medium bananas	3
1 tbsp.	lemon juice	15 mL
2 cups	strawberry ice cream	500 mL
1½ oz.	pkg. whipped topping	43 g
	whole maraschino cherries	
	chopped nuts	
	canned chocolate sauce OR fudge	
	sauce (see below)	

Prepare crumb crust and let cool. Slice bananas thinly and arrange in pie crust. Sprinkle lemon juice on bananas.

Stir ice cream to soften and then spread over bananas. Freeze until firm.

Prepare whipped topping as directed on package and spread over ice cream. Top with cherries and nuts. Return to freezer until firm.

About 30 minutes before serving time, remove pie from freezer and let stand at room temperature. To serve, drizzle each wedge with fudge sauce, see recipe below.

fudge sauce

yield: 1¾ cups (425 mL)

		90 mL
6 tbsp.	cocoa	175 mL
¾ cup	sugar	250 mL
1 cup	corn syrup	125 mL
½ cup	evaporated milk	1 mL
¼ tsp.	salt	30 mL
2 tbsp.	butter	2 mL
½ tsp.	vanilla	

Mix first 5 ingredients in a saucepan. Bring to a boil, stirring constantly. Cook and stir about 15 minutes (find yourself a good book!).

Remove from heat. Stir butter and vanilla into sauce.

note: This will thicken if stored in refrigerator, but no problem - just dilute with boiling water.

mud pie

yield: 10-12 servings

— go for it - it's from a Maui restaurant!

2 cups	Oreo cookie crumbs, about 20*	
4 cups	coffee ice cream OR chocolate	500 mL
½ cup	whipping cream	1 L
	sugar, to taste	125 mL
	vanilla, to taste	
½ cup	butterscotch syrup OR caramel	
		125 mL

Line a 9" (23 cm) pie plate with finely crushed cookie crumbs (they can be crushed by putting in a plastic bag and rolling with a rolling pin or whatever!). Reserve ¼ cup (50 mL) crumbs for topping - please. Freeze shell until firm, about 30 minutes.

Fill shell with softened ice cream and freeze again until firm.

Whip cream, flavor with a bit of sugar and vanilla and spread over ice cream. Top with cookie crumbs. Now — you guessed it — freeze until firm!

To serve, cut in wedges and drizzle with syrup.

* Cookie filling included.

102

popcorn balls

yield: 12 medium balls

		250 mL
1 cup	white sugar	75 mL
⅓ cup	white corn syrup OR yellow	75 mL
⅓ cup	water	50 mL
¼ cup	butter	3 mL
¾ tsp.	salt	3 mL
¾ tsp.	vanilla	3 L
3 quarts	popped corn (keep warm in oven at low temperature for best results)	

Combine first 5 ingredients in a heavy saucepan and cook until sugar is dissolved. Continue cooking without stirring until syrup forms a brittle ball in cold water (to test: just drop a few drops of syrup into a cup of cold water. Repeat until syrup forms a brittle ball).

Add vanilla. Pour syrup slowly over popped corn. Mix well. Grease hands and shape into balls.

note: Keep in airtight container.

baked caramel corn Ø

yield 6 quarts (6 L)

Preheat oven 250°F (120°C)

— what a treat! WARNING - it's addictive.

		250 mL
1 cup	butter	500 mL
2 cups	brown sugar	125 mL
½ cup	corn syrup	5 mL
1 tsp.	salt	2 mL
½ tsp.	baking soda	5 mL
1 tsp.	vanilla	6 L
6 quarts	popped corn	

Melt butter in a medium saucepan. Stir in brown sugar, corn syrup and salt. Bring to a boil and boil for 5 minutes. DO NOT STIR. Remove from heat and add baking soda and vanilla.

Put popped corn in a well-greased roaster. Gradually pour syrup over, stir well and bake 1 hour stirring every 15 minutes. Happy munching!

See photograph page 96A.

homemade poppycock

yield: 4½ quarts (4.5 L)

4 quarts	popped corn, unsalted	4 L
2 cups	mixed nuts	500 mL
3 cups	sugar	750 mL
1 cup	light corn syrup	250 mL
½ cup	water	125 mL
½ cup	butter	125 mL
1½ tsp.	salt	7 mL

Combine popcorn with nuts in large buttered bowl.

Combine remaining ingredients in heavy saucepan. Heat slowly until sugar melts. Cook to hard crack stage , 580°F (290°C) on candy thermometer.

Pour syrup slowly over popcorn, coating evenly. Spread on large buttered tray. Cool and break into chunks.

fudge

yield: 8 x 8" (20 x 20 cm) pan

5.5 oz.	Carnation evaporated milk	160 mL
1⅔ cups	white sugar	400 mL
½ tsp.	salt	2 mL
1 tsp.	vanilla	5 mL
½ cup	chopped nuts (optional)	125 mL
1½ cups	miniature marshmallows	375 mL
1½ cups	chocolate chipits	375 mL

Mix milk, sugar and salt in heavy saucepan. Heat to boiling, cook 5 minutes stirring constantly.

Remove from heat and add remaining ingredients.Stir until marshmallows dissolve.Pour into buttered 8 x 8" (20 x 20 cm) pan. Cool.

note: Doubling this recipe is not recommended.

index

vegetables

Recipes marked with Ø are easily halved - pan sizes and cooking times should be adjusted accordingly and writing in new measurements for all ingredients is advised.

Share *Cookbook for College Kids* with a friend.

Cookbook for College Kids is $12.95 per book/*Christmas Cooking for Santa* is $5.95 per book plus $3.00 (total order) for shipping and handling.

Cookbook for College Kids _____ x $12.95 = $ _____

Christmas Cooking for Santa _____ x $5.95 = $ _____

Postage and handling _____ = $ __3.00__

Subtotal _____ = $ _____

In Canada add 7% GST _____ (Subtotal x .07) = $ _____

Total enclosed _____ = $ _____

U.S. and international orders payable in U.S.funds./Price is subject to change.

NAME:_____

STREET:_____

CITY: _____ PROV. /STATE_____

COUNTRY _____ POSTAL CODE/ZIP_____

Please make cheque or
Money order payable to: **Cookbook for College Kids**
2207 Sirocco Drive S.W.
Calgary, Alberta
Canada   T3H 2T9

For fund raising or volume purchases, contact Cookbook for College Kids
for volume rates./Please allow 2-3 weeks for delivery.

Share *Cookbook for College Kids* with a friend.

Cookbook for College Kids is $12.95 per book/*Christmas Cooking for Santa* is $5.95 per book plus $3.00 (total order) for shipping and handling.

Cookbook for College Kids _____ x $12.95 = $ _____

Christmas Cooking for Santa _____ x $5.95 = $ _____

Postage and handling _____ = $ __3.00__

Subtotal _____ = $ _____

In Canada add 7% GST _____ (Subtotal x .07) = $ _____

Total enclosed _____ = $ _____

U.S. and international orders payable in U.S.funds./Price is subject to change.

NAME:_____

STREET:_____

CITY: _____ PROV. /STATE_____

COUNTRY _____ POSTAL CODE/ZIP_____

Please make cheque or
Money order payable to: **Cookbook for College Kids**
2207 Sirocco Drive S.W.
Calgary, Alberta
Canada   T3H 2T9

For fund raising or volume purchases, contact Cookbook for College Kids
for volume rates./Please allow 2-3 weeks for delivery.

Christmas Cooking for Santa
by Sheila McDougall, B.H.Sc.
Christmas Cooking for Santa is an ideal gift at Christmas – in Christmas baskets or Christmas stockings – printed in red and green it contains Christmas recipes and menus for the holiday season, from cookies, bars and squares to Treats for Tree Trimmers, a Christmas Eve Buffet, Christmas Morning Brunch, Christmas Dinner, a Boxing Day Buffet, a New Year's Buffet, and a storybook Gingerbread House. Christmas stories and anecdotes will put everyone in a festive mood.
Retail $5.95

48 pages

ISBN 0-919845-10-X

6" x 9"

line drawing

saddlestitched binding

Christmas Cooking for Santa
by Sheila McDougall, B.H.Sc.
Christmas Cooking for Santa is an ideal gift at Christmas – in Christmas baskets or Christmas stockings – printed in red and green it contains Christmas recipes and menus for the holiday season, from cookies, bars and squares to Treats for Tree Trimmers, a Christmas Eve Buffet, Christmas Morning Brunch, Christmas Dinner, a Boxing Day Buffet, a New Year's Buffet, and a storybook Gingerbread House. Christmas stories and anecdotes will put everyone in a festive mood.
Retail $5.95

48 pages

ISBN 0-919845-10-X

6" x 9"

line drawing

saddlestitched binding

Share *Cookbook for College Kids* with a friend.

Cookbook for College Kids is $12.95 per book/*Christmas Cooking for Santa* is $5.95 per book plus $3.00 (total order) for shipping and handling.

Cookbook for College Kids _____ x $12.95 = $ _____

Christmas Cooking for Santa _____ x $5.95 = $ _____

Postage and handling _____ = $ ___3.00___

Subtotal _____ = $ _____

In Canada add 7% GST _____(Subtotal x .07) = $ _____

Total enclosed _____ = $ _____

U.S. and international orders payable in U.S.funds./Price is subject to change.
_____

NAME: _____

STREET: _____

CITY: _____ PROV. /STATE _____

COUNTRY _____ POSTAL CODE/ZIP _____

Please make cheque or
Money order payable to: **Cookbook for College Kids**
2207 Sirocco Drive S.W.
Calgary, Alberta
Canada   T3H 2T9

For fund raising or volume purchases, contact Cookbook for College Kids
for volume rates./Please allow 2-3 weeks for delivery.

Share *Cookbook for College Kids* with a friend.

Cookbook for College Kids is $12.95 per book/*Christmas Cooking for Santa* is $5.95 per book plus $3.00 (total order) for shipping and handling.

Cookbook for College Kids _____ x $12.95 = $ _____

Christmas Cooking for Santa _____ x $5.95 = $ _____

Postage and handling _____ = $ ___3.00___

Subtotal _____ = $ _____

In Canada add 7% GST _____(Subtotal x .07) = $ _____

Total enclosed _____ = $ _____

U.S. and international orders payable in U.S.funds./Price is subject to change.

NAME: _____

STREET: _____

CITY: _____ PROV. /STATE _____

COUNTRY _____ POSTAL CODE/ZIP _____

Please make cheque or
Money order payable to: **Cookbook for College Kids**
2207 Sirocco Drive S.W.
Calgary, Alberta
Canada   T3H 2T9

For fund raising or volume purchases, contact Cookbook for College Kids
for volume rates./Please allow 2-3 weeks for delivery.

Christmas Cooking for Santa
by Sheila McDougall, B.H.Sc.
Christmas Cooking for Santa is an ideal gift at
Christmas – in Christmas baskets or Christmas
stockings – printed in red and green it contains
Christmas recipes and menus for the holiday
season, from cookies, bars and squares to
Treats for Tree Trimmers, a Christmas Eve
Buffet, Christmas Morning Brunch, Christmas
Dinner, a Boxing Day Buffet, a New Year's
Buffet, and a storybook Gingerbread House.
Christmas stories and anecdotes will put every-
one in a festive mood.
Retail $5.95

48 pages

ISBN 0-919845-10-X

6" x 9"

line drawing

saddlestitched binding

Christmas Cooking for Santa
by Sheila McDougall, B.H.Sc.
Christmas Cooking for Santa is an ideal gift at
Christmas – in Christmas baskets or Christmas
stockings – printed in red and green it contains
Christmas recipes and menus for the holiday
season, from cookies, bars and squares to
Treats for Tree Trimmers, a Christmas Eve
Buffet, Christmas Morning Brunch, Christmas
Dinner, a Boxing Day Buffet, a New Year's
Buffet, and a storybook Gingerbread House.
Christmas stories and anecdotes will put every-
one in a festive mood.
Retail $5.95

48 pages

ISBN 0-919845-10-X

6" x 9"

line drawing

saddlestitched binding